An Introduction to Source Analysis of the Pentateuch

AUXILIARY STUDIES IN THE BIBLE

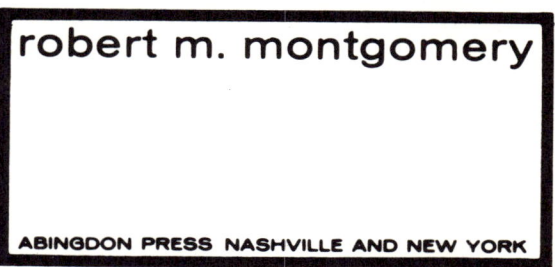

robert m. montgomery

ABINGDON PRESS NASHVILLE AND NEW YORK

AUXILIARY STUDIES IN THE BIBLE
AN INTRODUCTION TO SOURCE ANALYSIS OF THE PENTATEUCH

ISBN: 0-687-02325-4

Scripture quotations are from the Revised Standard Version
of the Bible, copyrighted 1946 and 1952 by the Division of
Christian Education, National Council of Churches, and are
used by permission.

                    Acknowledgments

The responses of many students in both college and seminary
          have made this program possible.
I wish gratefully to single out for special mention Miss
          Carol Jones and Mr. David Bucurel.
Professors Morgan Phillips, Richard Stegner, and LeGrand
          Tennis have been very helpful in their comments.
It is my wife who has brought the manuscript into its finished
          form.

          This program has been designed with verbal aptitudes
          ranging from 450 to 800 on the scale of the SAT. Students
          have scored high in the test on this unit devoting four to
          twelve hours to the use of this program, the amount of time
          being in proportion to verbal aptitudes.

72-2933

     Printed and bound by the Parthenon Press
at Nashville, Tennessee, United States of America

The following pages offer the student a *methodical way of learning*.
Do not treat the project as a test! You are not to hurry. Move along only
when you feel that you have absorbed the information in each frame.

Your attention will be directed to selected passages from the first five
books in the Old Testament. As certain passages are presented, you will be
introduced to the several aspects of a theory that attempts to solve the
puzzle of the several strands of thought in the Pentateuch. *Do not argue
with the presentation!* Any theory looks at evidence considered relevant in
a specific way. When at the end you understand how in the theory one views
the evidence cited, you may of course decide to reject or accept the theory.

Be sure to perform the tasks (check, draw lines, underline, etc.)
assigned to you in each frame. Since you will wish to check your responses
you can consult answers given either on the same page, or on the page following.
If it bothers you to have answers on the same page, simply cover them with
your arm or a piece of paper.

The goal of this unit:

    Having completed the unit and then answering questions and
    inspecting materials selected from the Pentateuch, the student
    should be able to identify the evidence supporting the theory
    that the Pentateuch is the work of at least four different
    schools of thought.

The next page presents an outline of the theory of sources for the Pentateuch.

Information

A theory about the authorship of the Pentateuch [the books of Genesis, Exodus, Leviticus, Numbers, and Deuteronomy] suggests that at least four different groups of thinkers produced the Pentateuch. The product of each group is called a "source" or "document." Accordingly the theory interprets the Pentateuch as a fabric of four interwoven layers of material from as many centuries.

The following names are commonly associated with each layer of material:

The Jahwist source was produced before 850 B.C.

The Elohist was written by 750 B.C.

The Deuteronomists published their view by 622/621 B.C.

The Priestly school of thought put the writings of the other schools together, adding its own point of view and thus producing the books that have been transmitted to us.

The evidence that more than one outlook is to be found in the Pentateuch requires some detective work. In the succeeding pages you will be mastering the evidence by analyzing the teachings that are expressed through stories, laws, and comments.

The programmed material does not require you to accept the theory; rather you are being trained in the way such a theory examines the varied material in the Pentateuch.

Now turn the page to begin the study of Source Analysis in the Pentateuch.

General observations are found in this box and often a suggestion about something you should think about or look for in material you are to examine:

In Jewish tradition, it was believed that one man had written the Pentateuch. Inspect the two examples of tradition and answer the questions below about the one believed to be the author of the five books.

In this box a quotation is given:

PIRKE ABOTH 1:1
   Moses received [when he wrote] the Law Torah from Sinai and transmitted to Joshua, Joshua to the elders, the elders to prophets, and the prophets transmitted to men of the Great Assembly...

MIDRASH GENESIS RABBAH VIII. 8
   Rabbi Samuel bar Nahman said in the name of Rabbi Jonathan: When Moses was engaged in writing the Torah, he wrote a portion each day. When he reached the Biblical verse that said: "And the LORD said, 'Let us make man in our image according to our likeness,'" [Moses] said: "Master of the Universe, why do you give an opening to heretics?" "Write," he answered, "for he who wishes to err, will err."

Commentary

PIRKE ABOTH *["Chapters" or "Lessons" of the Fathers] is one of the sections of the MISHNA. The MISHNA is a codification of Jewish law published in its definitive edition around 200 A.D.*

MIDRASH GENESIS RABBAH *is produced possibly in the sixth century A.D., but it contains much early material.*

The Hebrew term TORAH *is much broader than the English word "law." TORAH means "Teaching" or "Revelation." Generally TORAH is the name given to the Pentateuch, and that is its meaning in both quotations here.*

"an opening." *The language will suggest to the heretic that there is more than one God.*

In this box some tasks are set for you:

Place a check before the element that correctly completes each statement.

   1. Pirke Aboth records an important tradition that two versions of the Torah [one written and the other oral] were received at Sinai. But the important matter for us--it is thought that God gave the Torah to

   ___ a. Moses.

   ___ b. Moses indirectly, but Joshua received the Torah directly.

   ___ c. Joshua indirectly, but the men of the Great Assembly received the Torah directly from God.

   2. The passage from Midrash Genesis Rabbah

   ___ a. disagrees with Pirke Aboth; it was Rabbi Jonathan who wrote the Torah.
   ___ b. agrees with Pirke Aboth that Moses received the Torah from God.

Now you check your answers given, in this case, on the next page.————————▶

1. Pirke Aboth records an important tradition that two versions of the Torah [one written and the other oral] were received at Sinai. But the important matter for us--it is thought that God gave the Torah to

   ✔ a. Moses.

   ___ b. Moses indirectly, but Joshua received the Torah directly.

   ___ c. Joshua indirectly, but the men of the Great Assembly received the Torah directly from God.

2. The passage from Midrash Genesis Rabbah

   ___ a. disagrees with Pirke Aboth; it was Rabbi Jonathan who wrote the Torah.

   ✔ b. agrees with Pirke Aboth that Moses received the Torah from God.

Inspect the Christian passages below to discover early Christian assumptions on the *authorship* of the Torah. The passages quoted below all come from the New Testament.

Acts 3:22. Moses said, "The Lord God will raise up for you a prophet from your brethren as he raised me up..."	*Commentary* *The book of Acts gives us the early development of Christianity to a point before the death of Paul [64? A.D.]. Deuteronomy 18:15 is being quoted.*
Romans 10:5. Moses writes that the man who practices the righteousness which is based on the law shall live by it.	*Paul wrote Romans and the letters to the Corinthian church.* *The passage from Romans uses Leviticus 18:5.*
I Corinthians 9:9. For it is written in the law of Moses, "You shall not muzzle an ox when it is treading out the grain."	*Paul in this passage quotes Deuteronomy 25:4.*

Circle the number of any correct statement below.

1. If the works quoted above are typical, Christian tradition thought that Moses had written the Pentateuch.

2. So Christian tradition disagrees with Jewish tradition about the authorship of the Torah.

3. And Christian tradition agrees with Jewish tradition about the authorship of the Pentateuch.

ANSWER to Frame # 2

1 and 3 are correct.

The frame on this page tells us whether or not in the New Testament it is thought that Moses wrote the Pentateuch.
The next frame will reveal whether in Old Testament times it was thought that Moses wrote the Torah.

Note the tradition about the Torah in the fifth century B.C. and answer the questions below.

Nehemiah 8:1-3.

And all the people gathered as one man into the square before the Water Gate; and they told Ezra the scribe to bring the book of the law [*Torah* in the Hebrew] of Moses which the LORD had given to Israel. And Ezra the priest brought the law before the assembly, both men and women and all who could hear with understanding, on the first day of the seventh month. And he read from it facing the square before the Water Gate from early morning until midday, in the presence of the men and the women and those who could understand; and the ears of all the people were attentive to the book of the law.

Commentary

This account, though found in the book of Nehemiah, appears to belong to the story of Ezra. The latter seems to have returned to Palestine from Babylon later than Nehemiah who helped the returned exiles to organize about the middle of the fifth century.

Ezra becomes the center of a movement to focus the life of the community on obedience to the Torah.

Cross out the statements below that give an inaccurate analysis of the tradition about the authorship of the Torah.

1. Since it was too late to organize an objective study of the authorship of the Pentateuch, the tradition frankly admits that the author[s] of Genesis, Exodus, Leviticus, Numbers, and Deuteronomy is [are] unknown.

2. The view that Moses gave the Torah to his people is early enough to be found in the Old Testament itself.

3. The idea that Moses wrote the Torah thus is a contribution of Christian tradition alone.

4. The Jewish and the Christian tradition did not invent the idea that Moses wrote the Torah, for this concept came to them from the Scriptures they both read.

ANSWER to Frame # 3

l and 3 should be crossed out.

Information

We are not primarily concerned with following through the course of the tradition that Moses wrote the Pentateuch, but you may find the following of interest.

Some writers in the Christian tradition took seriously an additional note on the authorship of the Pentateuch. In a work published possibly as late as 120 A.D., one finds the idea that Ezra, the scribe mentioned in Frame # 3, repeated the miraculous assembly of the Pentateuch.

In this work, called IV EZRA, we find a voice speaking out of a bush to Ezra. [There is an episode like this in the stories about Moses.] Ezra is worried that the Torah has been destroyed, you see. So the voice from the bush, the voice of God, commands Ezra to bring together five secretaries who are good at taking dictation. Then after Ezra has drunk a cup of a liquid, "the cup of inspiration," Ezra pours forth the whole of the Old Testament [not just the Torah] in forty days and nights.[1]

[1]You may wish to read this account in the following publication: *The Apocrypha and Pseudepigrapha of the Old Testament*. Volume II, *Pseudepigrapha*, Oxford, 1913. *IV Ezra*, translation and commentary by G. H. Box, pp. 542-624. The account I have summarized is found in chapter 14:1-7,21-48.

We turn now to reasons why some scholars do not accept the tradition that Moses wrote the Pentateuch.

Examine the passage below to find data for a simple objection to the idea that Moses wrote *all* the Torah.

Deuteronomy 34:4-6. [Chapter 34 is the last chapter in Deuteronomy.]

   And the LORD said to him, "This is the land of which I swore to Abraham, to Isaac, and to Jacob, 'I will give it to your descendants.' I have let you see it with your eyes, but you shall not go over there." So Moses the servant of the LORD died there in the land of Moab, according to the word of the LORD, and he buried him in the valley in the land of Moab opposite Beth-peor; but no man knows the place of his burial to this day.

Place a check before elements that complete logically each statement below.

   1. If someone were examining this body of literature in the same way that
      he studied any other body of writing he would suppose that

      ____ a. a person would be able to write the story of his own death.

      ____ b. a person whose death is recounted would not have written at
             least the story of his own death.

   2. The phrase "no man knows the place of his burial to this day" suggests

      ____ a. only that Moses did not wish his tomb to be honored.

      ____ b. that events are being recorded at a time much later than the
             one in which the events occurred.

ANSWER to Frame # 4

   1. b   2. b

Here is evidence more significant than the story of the death of Moses. Examine the passages below to find the names used for the deity.

P. Passages taken from Genesis 1:1 - 2:4a. [Assigned to the Priestly source = P]

   1:1. In the beginning God created the heavens and the earth.

   1:3. And God said, "Let there be light"; and there was light.

   1:10. God called the dry land Earth, and the waters that were gathered
         together he called Seas.

   1:14. And God said, "Let there be lights in the firmament of the heavens
         to separate the day from the night; and let them be for signs and for
         seasons and for days and years..."

   2:2. And on the seventh day God finished his work which he had done, and
        he rested on the seventh day from all his work which he had done.

J. Passages taken from Genesis 2:4b - 3:24. [Assigned to the Jahwist = J]

   2:4b. In the day that the LORD God made the earth and the heavens...

   2:7. ...then the LORD God formed man of dust from the ground, and
        breathed into his nostrils the breath of life; and man became a
        living being.

   2:18. Then the LORD God said, "It is not good that the man should be
         alone; I will make him a helper fit for him."

   2:21,22. So the LORD God caused a deep sleep to fall upon the man, and
         while he slept took one of his ribs and closed up its place with flesh;
         and the rib which the LORD God had taken from the man he made into a
         woman and brought her to the man.

   3:8. And they heard the sound of the LORD God walking in the garden in
        the cool of the day, and the man and his wife hid themselves from the
        presence of the LORD God among the trees of the garden.

Inspecting the passages above, indicate below if a statement describes either
group of passages, placing checks appropriately. For example: statement no. 1
does not describe either P or J so it is left unchecked.

   P   J
   ___ ___ 1. Most of the time "God" is used, and only once is "LORD God"
           employed.

   ___ ___ 2. Most of the time "LORD God" appears, and only once is "God"
           used.

   ___ ___ 3. The term "God" is used exclusively.

   ___ ___ 4. The term "LORD God" is the only one appearing.

ANSWER to Frame # 5

P   J

_____ _____ 1. Most of the time "God" is used, and only once is "LORD God" employed.

_____ _____ 2. Most of the time "LORD God" appears, and only once is "God" used.

✓ _____ 3. The term "God" is used exclusively.

_____ ✓ 4. The term "LORD God" is the only one appearing.

Frame # 6

In order to explore differences between the terms "God" and "LORD God," it is useful to learn how to use distinctions between ways of referring to a Supreme Being.

A. One can use *generic* terms. Such a term includes any kind of Supreme Being.

B. One can use terms that identify the *specific* deity that one worships.

Now classify the terms below by circling the class appropriate to each term.

[Generic]   [Specific]   1. god.

[Generic]   [Specific]   2. Zeus.

[Generic]   [Specific]   3. The One who revealed himself only
                            in Jesus the Christ.

[Generic]   [Specific]   4. Thor.

[Generic]   [Specific]   5. Jupiter.

[Generic]   [Specific]   6. Venus.

ANSWER to Frame # 6

([Generic]) [Specific]   1. god.

[Generic] ([Specific])   2. Zeus.

[Generic] ([Specific])   3. The One who revealed himself only
                              in Jesus the Christ.

[Generic] ([Specific])   4. Thor.

[Generic] ([Specific])   5. Jupiter.

[Generic] ([Specific])   6. Venus.

You need the following information in order to make the classifications in the passages below.

One of the Hebrew words for *God* is "Elohim," and the Hebrew term for the name of the God <u>worshipped by the Israelites was "Jahweh."</u> A special tradition developed which dictated that one substituted the word "Lord" for the term "Jahweh."

So by means of a simple code in the English translation it is possible for us to know what word is used in the Hebrew; when the name "Jahweh" appears in the Hebrew, whether Jahweh is rendered by "Lord" or by "God" <u>every letter in the English terms is capitalized.</u>

The following table will help you in the tasks below.

Hebrew	English translation in this Unit
Adon [*Lord*]* ------------------------------	Lord
Lord Jahweh ----------------------------	Lord GOD
Jahweh Elohim ----------------------------	LORD God
Jahweh [by itself] ------------------	LORD
Elohim ----------------------------------	God

Below on the left side you find the terms which might be occurring in the Hebrew. On the right side you find passages in the English translation. Indicate the correct classification of each reference to the deity by listing the number with the appropriate term in the left-hand column. For example, no. 2 below represents "Jahweh Elohim."

Lord __ __ __   In the beginning $\overset{1}{\text{God}}$ created the heavens...

Lord Jahweh __ __ __   ...then the $\overset{2}{\text{LORD God}}$ formed man of dust from...

Jahweh Elohim _2_ __ __   And on the seventh day $\overset{3}{\text{God}}$ finished his work...

Jahweh [by itself] __ __ __   O $\overset{4}{\text{Lord}}$, let the $\overset{5}{\text{Lord}}$, I pray thee, go in the...

Elohim __ __ __   ...the $\overset{6}{\text{LORD}}$, a $\overset{7}{\text{God}}$ merciful and gracious,...

But Abram said, "O $\overset{8}{\text{Lord GOD}}$, what wilt thou give..."

Underline the correct choices in the statement below.

"Elohim" is a (generic)(specific) term for the deity, while "Jahweh" is a (generic)(specific) term.

---

* We will not concern ourselves further with the Hebrew word "adon."

Lord _4_ _5_ __

Lord Jahweh _8_ __ __

Jahweh Elohim _2_ __ __

Jahweh [by itself] _6_ __ __

Elohim _1_ _3_ _7_

In the beginning $\overline{\text{God}}^{1}$ created the heavens...

...then the $\overline{\text{LORD God}}^{2}$ formed man of dust from...

And on the seventh day $\overline{\text{God}}^{3}$ finished his work...

O $\overline{\text{Lord}}^{4}$, let the $\overline{\text{Lord}}^{5}$, I pray thee, go in the...

...the $\overline{\text{LORD}}^{6}$, a $\overline{\text{God}}^{7}$ merciful and gracious,...

But Abram said, "O $\overline{\text{Lord GOD}}^{8}$, what wilt thou give..."

Underline the correct choices in the statements below.

"Elohim" is a (generic)(specific) term for the deity, while "Jahweh" is a (generic)(specific) term.

Exhibit for Frame # 8

Instructions for the use of this exhibit will be found on the opposite page.

P. Passages taken from Genesis 1:1 - 2:4a. = the Priestly source.

1:1. In the beginning God created the heavens and the earth.

1:3. And God said, "Let there be light"; and there was light.

1:10. God called the dry land Earth, and the waters that were gathered together he called Seas.

1:14. And God said, "Let there be lights in the firmament of the heavens to separate the day from the night; and let them be for signs and for seasons and for days and years..."

2:2. And on the seventh day God finished his work which he had done, and he rested on the seventh day from all his work which he had done.

J. Passages taken from Genesis 2:4b - 3:24.= the Jahwist source.

2:4b. In the day that the LORD God made the earth and the heavens...

2:7. ...then the LORD God formed man of dust from the ground, and breathed into his nostrils the breath of life; and man became a living being.

2:18. Then the LORD God said, "It is not good that the man should be alone; I will make him a helper fit for him."

2:21,22. So the LORD God caused a deep sleep to fall upon the man, and while he slept took one of his ribs and closed up its place with flesh; and the rib which the LORD God had taken from the man he made into a woman and brought her to the man.

3:8. And they heard the sound of the LORD God walking in the garden in the cool of the day, and the man and his wife hid themselves from the presence of the LORD God among the trees of the garden.

We examine again the comparison between selected portions of Genesis 1:1-2:4a and **Genesis 2:4b-3:24. Employ the distinctions you have practiced in order to** answer the questions about the passages given on the opposite page in the exhibit.

Below are clauses making generalizations about the terms used for the deity in the collections labeled "P" and "J." Select the <u>correct</u> generalizations by placing checks appropriately.

For example: Inspection of the Priestly material given in the exhibit shows that clause "b" under "1" states correctly that the Priestly passages use the Hebrew word Elohim.

    1. The passages taken from Genesis 1:1-2:4a.

        ____ a. use the Hebrew word Elohim;

        ____ b. use the Hebrew words Elohim and Jahweh;

        ____ c. use the Hebrew word Jahweh;

        ____ d. and thus use a generic term for God exclusively.

        ____ e. and thus use both a generic term and a specific name.

    2. The passages taken from Genesis 2:4b-3:24.

        ____ a. use Jahweh Elohim for God;

        ____ b. use exclusively Elohim for God;

        ____ c. consequently <u>do not</u> identify the God as a specific one.

        ____ d. consequently <u>do</u> identify the God as a specific one; in other words they identify the deity by name.

1. The passages taken from Genesis 1:1-2:4a.

    _✓_ a. use the Hebrew word Elohim;

    ___ b. use the Hebrew words Elohim and Jahweh;

    ___ c. use the Hebrew word Jahweh;

    _✓_ d. and thus use a generic term for God exclusively.

    ___ e. and thus use both a generic term and a specific name.

2. The passages taken from Genesis 2:4b-3:24.

    _✓_ a. use Jahweh Elohim for God;

    ___ b. use exclusively Elohim for God;

    ___ c. consequently <u>do</u> <u>not</u> identify the God as a specific one.

    _✓_ d. consequently <u>do</u> identify the God as a specific one; in other words they identify the deity by name.

We move on now to see whether differences in ideas accompany differences in terms.

Be alert to the possible theoretical differences among *activities* of the deity in the P and J passages below.

P. Genesis 1:3. And God <u>said</u>, "Let there be light"; and there was light.
    1:10. God <u>called</u> the dry land Earth, and the waters that were gathered together he <u>called</u> Seas.

J. Genesis 2:7. ...then the LORD God <u>formed</u> man of dust from the ground, and <u>breathed</u> into his nostrils the breath of life; and man became a living being.
    2:21,22. So the LORD God caused a deep sleep to fall upon the man, and while he slept <u>took</u> one of his ribs and <u>closed up</u> its place with flesh; and the rib which the LORD God had taken from the man he made into a woman and <u>brought</u> her to the man.

Below three groups of terms are found in each question; draw lines so that the sentences produced accurately describe the differences between the Priestly and the Jahwist sources in the conception of the deity. For example see the first part of the first question.

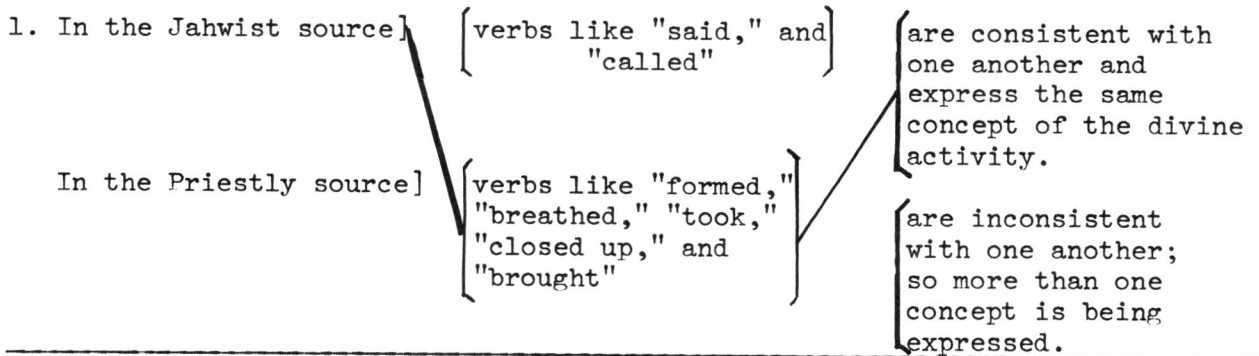

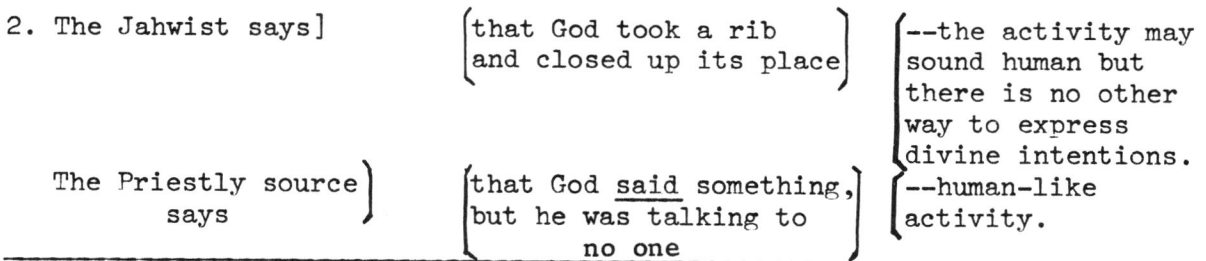

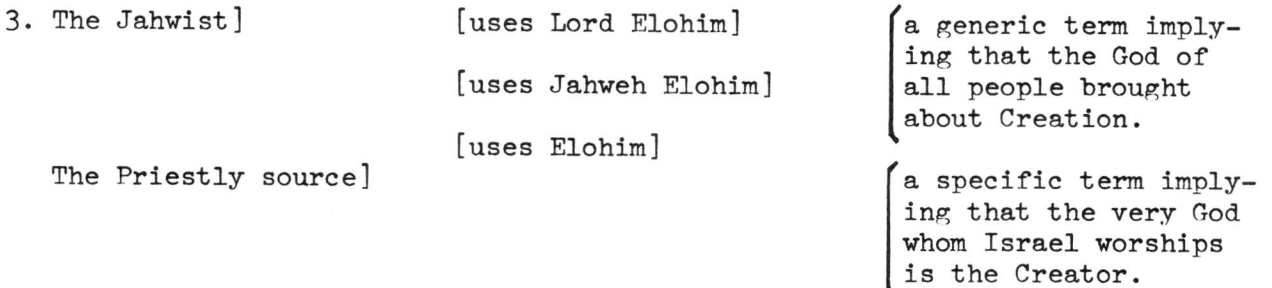

1. In the Jahwist source]
   In the Priestly source]

   [verbs like "said," and "called"

   [verbs like "formed," "breathed," "took," "closed up," and "brought"

   {are consistent with one another and express the same concept of the divine activity.

   {are inconsistent with one another; so more than one concept is being expressed.

2. The Jahwist says]
   The Priestly source says)

   {that God took a rib and closed up its place

   {that God <u>said</u> something, but he was talking to no one

   {--the activity may sound human but there is no other way to express divine intentions.
   {--human-like activity.

3. The Jahwist]
   The Priestly source]

   [uses Lord Elohim]
   [uses Jahweh Elohim]
   [uses Elohim]

   {a generic term implying that the God of all people brought about Creation.

   {a specific term implying that the very God whom Israel worships is the Creator.

ANSWER to Frame # 9

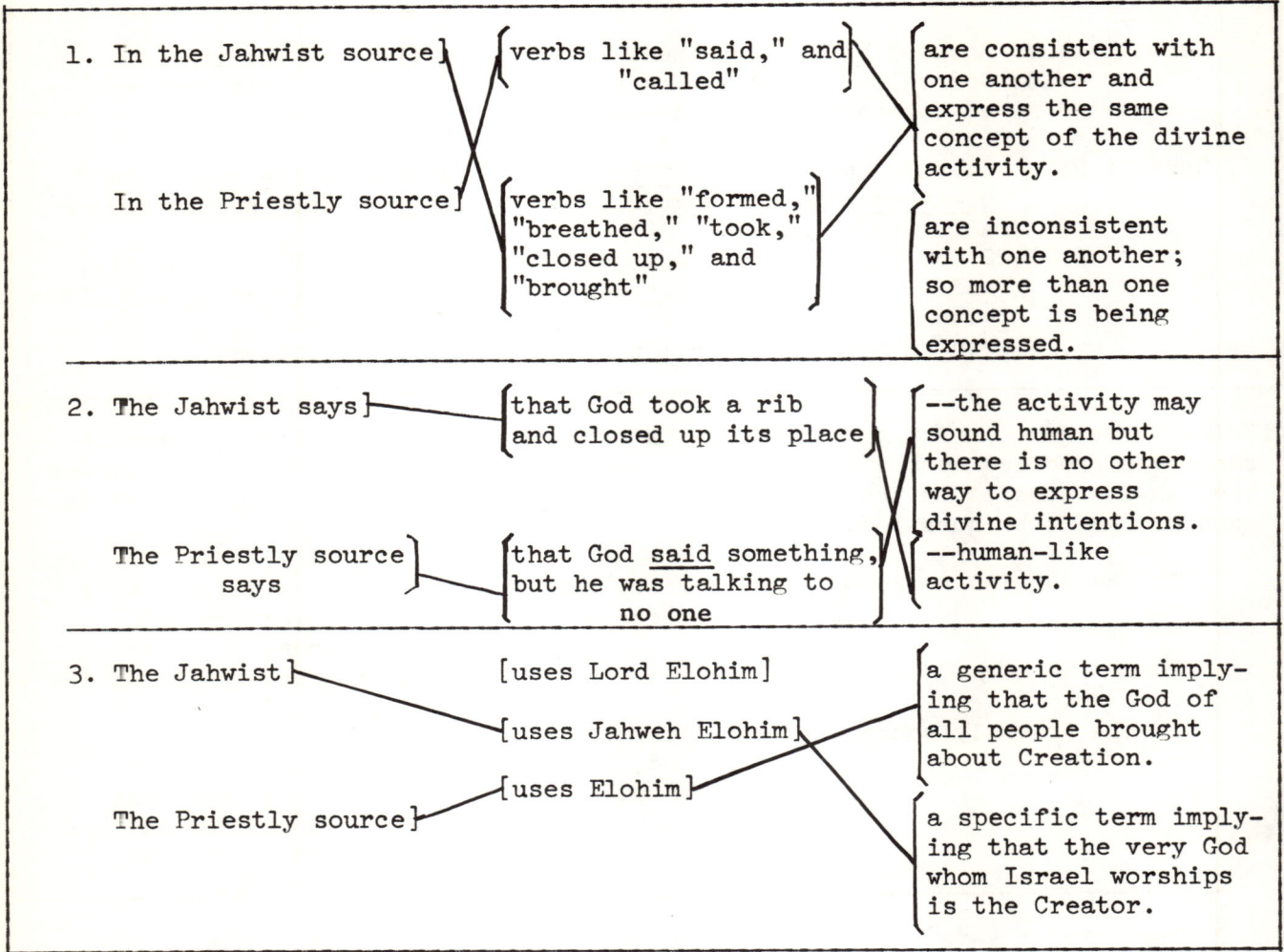

1. In the Jahwist source ⟩   ⟨ verbs like "said," and "called" ⟩   ⟨ are consistent with one another and express the same concept of the divine activity.

   In the Priestly source ⟩   ⟨ verbs like "formed," "breathed," "took," "closed up," and "brought" ⟩   ⟨ are inconsistent with one another; so more than one concept is being expressed.

2. The Jahwist says ⟩   ⟨ that God took a rib and closed up its place ⟩   ⟨ --the activity may sound human but there is no other way to express divine intentions. --human-like activity.

   The Priestly source says ⟩   ⟨ that God said something, but he was talking to no one ⟩

3. The Jahwist ⟩   [uses Lord Elohim]   ⟨ a generic term implying that the God of all people brought about Creation.

   [uses Jahweh Elohim]

   The Priestly source ⟩   [uses Elohim]   ⟨ a specific term implying that the very God whom Israel worships is the Creator.

In responding to the questions in a frame be sure to reason out the answer from the evidence given.

Examine one more Jahwist passage to see the extent of the human-like aspects of the deity.

Genesis 3:8-10.

And they heard the sound of the LORD God walking in the garden in the cool of the day, and the man and his wife hid themselves from the presence of the LORD God among the trees of the garden. But the LORD God called to the man, and said to him, "Where are you?" And he said, "I heard the sound of thee in the garden, and I was afraid, because I was naked; and I hid myself."

1. Write the Hebrew terms for the deity used in this section.

_____   _____.

Now we concern ourselves with the probable conclusions of someone who is reading Genesis in the same way that he studies any other literature. Underline the more probable elements in the following statements.

2. The expression that "they heard the sound of the LORD God walking" suggests that the deity's walk could be identified by its sound. A reader could conclude that this way of writing expresses (non-human-like)(human-like) activities.

3. It is also said that the LORD God takes a walk "in the cool of the day." Bearing in mind that the Bible comes from a warm climate, a reader could conclude that the deity's activities are thought of as (very much like that of a man)(quite unlike that of a man).

4. The man and his wife hid from the LORD God. It seems that (the deity's eyesight is limited in vision as is man's)(the man and his wife do not yet possess human qualities, for they cannot yet be seen).

5. A further exploration of the significance of hiding from God--(the deity cannot see the man and his wife; so he has to call them)(the language is not meant literally because the deity can see them and speaks to them without having to ask them where they are).

6. This passage encourages the reader to make a conclusion about the way in which the writer thinks about the deity. (The writer deliberately avoids describing the deity's activities in ways that might be misunderstood as human-like.) (The writer appears to think of the deity as possessing human or human-like characteristics.)

1. Write the Hebrew terms for the deity used in this section.

   Jahweh   _Elohim_ .

2. The expression that "they heard the <u>sound</u> of the LORD God walking" suggests that the deity's <u>walk</u> could be identified by its sound. A reader could conclude that this way of writing expresses (non-human-like)(<u>human-like</u>) activities.

3. It is also said that the LORD God takes a walk "in the cool of the day." Bearing in mind that the Bible comes from a warm climate, a reader could conclude that the deity's activities are thought of as (<u>very much like that of a man</u>)(quite unlike that of a man).

4. The man and his wife <u>hid</u> from the LORD God. It seems that (<u>the deity's eyesight is limited in vision as is man's</u>)(the man and his wife do not yet possess human qualities, for they cannot yet be seen).

5. A further exploration of the significance of <u>hiding</u> from God--(<u>the deity cannot see the man and his wife; so he has to call them</u>)(the language is not meant literally because the deity can see them and speaks to them without having to ask them where they are).

5. This passage encourages the reader to make a conclusion about the way in which the writer thinks about the deity.
   (The writer deliberately <u>avoids</u> describing the deity's activities in ways that might be misunderstood as human-like.)
   (<u>The writer appears to think of the deity as possessing human or human-like characteristics.</u>)

Instructions for the use of this exhibit will be found on the opposite page.

P. Genesis 1:14-18. And God said, "Let there be lights in the firmament of the heavens to separate the day from the night; and let them be for signs and for seasons and for days and years, and let them be lights in the firmament of the heavens to give light upon the earth." And it was so. And God made the two great lights, the greater light to rule the day, and the lesser light to rule the night; he made the stars also. And God set them in the firmament of the heavens to give light upon the earth, to rule over the day and over the night, and to separate the light from the darkness. And God saw that it was good. And there was evening and there was morning, a fourth day.

Genesis 1:24-27. And God said, "Let the earth bring forth living creatures according to their kinds: cattle and creeping things and beasts of the earth according to their kinds." And it was so. And God made the beasts of the earth according to their kinds and the cattle according to their kinds, and everything that creeps upon the ground according to its kind. And God saw that it was good.
Then God said, "Let us make man in our image, after our likeness; and let them have dominion over the fish of the sea, and over the birds of the air, and over the cattle, and over all the earth, and over every creeping thing that creeps upon the earth."
So God created man in his own image, in the image of God he created him; male and female he created them.

Genesis 1:31. And God saw everything that he had made, and behold, it was very good. And there was evening and there was morning, a sixth day.

J. Genesis 2:18-22. Then the LORD God said, "It is not good that the man should be alone; I will make him a helper fit for him." So out of the ground the LORD God formed every beast of the field and every bird of the air, and brought them to the man to see what he would call them; and whatever the man called every living creature, that was its name. The man gave names to all cattle, and to the birds of the air, and to every beast of the field; but for the man there was not found a helper fit for him. So the LORD God caused a deep sleep to fall upon the man, and while he slept took one of his ribs and closed up its place with flesh; and the rib which the LORD God had taken from the man he made into a woman and brought her to the man.

Genesis 3:21-23. And the LORD God made for Adam and for his wife garments of skins, and clothed them. Then the LORD God said, "Behold, the man has become like one of us, knowing good and evil; and now, lest he put forth his hand and take also of the tree of life, and eat, and live for ever" --therefore the LORD God sent him forth from the garden of Eden, to till the ground from which he was taken.

Below statements are made about the passages from the Priestly and the Jahwist sources quoted in the exhibit on the opposite page.
Assign the statements to the appropriate source by placing either a "P" or a "J" in the blank preceding each statement.

____ 1. By portraying the deity in human terms the source can accent the deep involvement of the deity in his human creation.

____ 2. It would appear that the creation of animals comes about because the deity has noticed that man needs a companion.

____ 3. The deity anticipates the needs of companionship by creating male and female at the same time.

____ 4. The chief interest in this story of Creation centers in man.

____ 5. The deity is so close to his human creation that he is portrayed as having made clothes for Adam and his wife.

____ 6. A certain stateliness and dignity permeates this account of Creation, a stateliness accentuated by the repetition of key phrases.

____ 7. This account of Creation accents the plan and foreknowledge of the deity; he does not discover things and then add to his Creation.

____ 8. It is emphasized that nature which God has created is good; it is not an evil world that the deity considers to be in contradiction to himself.

J 1. By portraying the deity in human terms the source can accent the deep involvement of the deity in his human creation.

J 2. It would appear that the creation of animals comes about because the deity has noticed that man needs a companion.

P 3. The deity anticipates the needs of companionship by creating male and female at the same time.

J 4. The chief interest in this story of Creation centers in man.

J 5. The deity is so close to his human creation that he is portrayed as having made clothes for Adam and his wife.

P 6. A certain stateliness and dignity permeates this account of Creation, a stateliness accentuated by the repetition of key phrases.

P 7. This account of Creation accents the plan and foreknowledge of the deity; he does not discover things and then add to his Creation.

P 8. It is emphasized that nature which God has created is good; it is not an evil world that the deity considers to be in contradiction to himself.

Exhibit for Frame # 12

Instructions for the use of this exhibit will be found on the opposite page.

A. Genesis 6:5-7.

The LORD saw that the wickedness of man was great in the earth, and that every imagination of the thoughts of his heart was only evil continually. And the LORD was sorry that he had made man on the earth, and it grieved him to his heart. So the LORD said, "I will blot out man whom I have created from the face of the ground, man and beast and creeping things and birds of the air, for I am sorry that I have made them."

B. Genesis 7:1-3.

Then the LORD said to Noah, "Go into the ark, you and all your house-hold, for I have seen that you are righteous before me in this gener-ation. Take with you seven pairs of all clean animals, the male and his mate; and a pair of the animals that are not clean, the male and his mate; and seven pairs of the birds of the air also, male and female, to keep their kind alive upon the face of all the earth."

C. Genesis 6:19. And of every living thing of all flesh, you shall bring two of every sort into the ark, to keep them alive with you; they shall be male and female. Genesis 7:8,9. Of clean animals, and of animals that are not clean, and of birds, and of everything that creeps on the ground, two and two, male and female, went into the ark with Noah, as God had commanded Noah.

D. Genesis 8:20,21.

Then Noah built an altar to the LORD, and took of every clean animal and of every clean bird, and offered burnt offerings on the altar. And when the LORD smelled the pleasing odor, the LORD said in his heart, "I will never again curse the ground because of man, for the imagination of man's heart is evil from his youth; neither will I ever again destroy every living creature as I have done."

Differences in terms referring to the deity, differences in ideas about the deity, differences in the stories of Creation--examine the passages in the exhibit for another difference.

The Number of Animals in the Ark.

1. When "B" and "C" are inspected, one can see that

___ a. the accounts agree because only a pair of every kind of animal is taken into the ark.

___ b. the accounts disagree, for in "B" there are seven pairs of clean animals and one pair of unclean, while in "C" one pair each of both clean and unclean animals were taken into the ark.

2. When the account "D" is added to "B" and "C"

___ a. there is no problem because "D" would go along with either "C" or "B."

___ b. there is a problem because clean animals are sacrificed in "D," but in "C" there is only one pair of clean animals so there would be no mate left to propagate the species. Thus "D" could only be matched with "B" where there are seven pairs.

Terms used for the Deity.

3. Circle below the letters of the selections that use the specific name for the deity.

A   B   C   D

4. Circle below the letters of the selections that use the generic name for the deity.

A   B   C   D

1. When "B" and "C" are inspected, one can see that

    ___ a. the accounts agree because only a pair of every kind of
    animal is taken into the ark.

    ✓ b. the accounts disagree, for in "B" there are seven pairs of
    clean animals and one pair of unclean, while in "C" one pair each
    of both clean and unclean animals were taken into the ark.

2. When the account "D" is added to "B" and "C"

    ___ a. there is no problem because "D" would go along with either
    "C" or "B."

    ✓ b. there is a problem because clean animals are sacrificed in
    "D," but in "C" there is only one pair of clean animals so
    there would be no mate left to propagate the species. Thus
    "D" could only be matched with "B" where there are seven pairs.

3. Circle below the letters of the selections that use the specific
name for the deity.

    Ⓐ   Ⓑ   C   Ⓓ

4. Circle below the letters of the selections that use the generic
name for the deity.

    A   B   Ⓒ   D

Instructions for the use of this exhibit will be found on the opposite page.

A. Genesis 6:5-7.

The LORD saw that the wickedness of man was great in the earth, and
that every imagination of the thoughts of his heart was only evil
continually. And the LORD was sorry that he had made man on the earth,
and it grieved him to his heart. So the LORD said, "I will blot out
man whom I have created from the face of the ground, man and beast and
creeping things and birds of the air, for I am sorry that I have made
them."

B. Genesis 7:1-3.

Then the LORD said to Noah, "Go into the ark, you and all your household, for I have seen that you are righteous before me in this generation. Take with you seven pairs of all clean animals, the male and
his mate; and a pair of the animals that are not clean, the male and
his mate; and seven pairs of the birds of the air also, male and female,
to keep their kind alive upon the face of all the earth."

C. Genesis 6:19. And of every living thing of all flesh, you shall bring
two of every sort into the ark, to keep them alive with you; they
shall be male and female. Genesis 7:8,9. Of clean animals, and of
animals that are not clean, and of birds, and of everything that creeps
on the ground, two and two, male and female, went into the ark with
Noah, as God had commanded Noah.

D. Genesis 8:20,21.

Then Noah built an altar to the LORD, and took of every clean animal
and of every clean bird, and offered burnt offerings on the altar.
And when the LORD smelled the pleasing odor, the LORD said in his heart,
"I will never again curse the ground because of man, for the imagination
of man's heart is evil from his youth; neither will I ever again destroy
every living creature as I have done."

The exhibit from the previous frame has been repeated so that you can identify which of the passages belong to the Jahwist and which belong to the Priestly source.

You have identified which of the passages use the specific name of the deity.

1. With respect to language about God that employs distinctly human-like terms, the Jahwist showed

   ___ a. no reluctance about such terms.

   ___ b. a rejection of such terms, for only elevated symbolic language was used for the description of divine activities.

2. Now the task is to identify the passages that *clearly* imply either human emotions or the possibility of a human shape for the deity.

   In "B" we find "the LORD said" and in "D" the phrasing "as God had commanded."

   There is no special religious vocabulary except for the word "God." If a passage uses the words "said" and "commanded,"

   ___ a. whether a human-like shape is implied is not clear.

   ___ b. a human-like shape is intended clearly.

3. Examine "A" and "D" for evidence of language that implies either human emotions or the possibility of a human shape for the deity.

   What expressions do you find in "A?" _____

   _____

   What expressions do you find in "D?" _____

   _____

4. Considering the matter of human-like language if appropriate, and the names for the deity, circle the letters of the sections that belong to the Jahwist.

   A   B   C   D

5. Considering the matter of human-like language if appropriate, and the names for the deity, circle the letters of the sections that belong to the Priestly source.

   A   B   C   D

1. With respect to language about God that employs distinctly human-like terms, the Jahwist showed

   ✓ a. no reluctance about such terms.

   ___ b. a rejection of such terms, for only elevated symbolic language was used for the description of divine activities.

2. Now the task is to identify the passages that *clearly* imply either human emotions or the possibility of a human shape for the deity.

   In "B" we find "the LORD said" and in "D" the phrasing "as God had commanded."

   There is no special religious vocabulary except for the word "God." If a passage uses the words "said" and "commanded,"

   ✓ a. whether a human-like shape is implied is not clear.

   ___ b. a human-like shape is intended clearly.

3. Examine "A" and "D" for evidence of language that implies either human emotions or the possibility of a human shape for the deity.

   Students have noted the following expressions.

   A. *Jahweh was "sorry" and "grieved," human-like emotions assigned to the deity.*

   D. *Jahweh is described as having "smelled" the odor of the sacrifice, language that implies nostrils and therefore a human shape for the deity.*

4. Considering the matter of human-like language if appropriate, and the names for the deity, circle the letters of the sections that belong to the Jahwist.

   Ⓐ   Ⓑ   C   Ⓓ

5. Considering the matter of human-like language if appropriate, and the names for the deity, circle the letters of the sections that belong to the Priestly source.

   A   B   Ⓒ   D

By now you should know why certain scholars think of the Pentateuch as having been produced by more than one author.

Since the Priestly source is thought of as having come last we will return to it later in this programmed unit.

A. This account from a Babylonian epic called the Gilgamesh Epic was written
in the seventh century B.C.

[The hero of this episode has been informed that there is to be a flood
and that he should build a ship. When he has boarded the ship with his
kin, some craftsmen, and animals, the great rainstorm began.]

114. The gods were frightened at the deluge,
115. They fled, they climbed to the highest heaven;
116. The gods crouched like dogs, they lay down by the walls.

[For seven days and nights it rained. Then as the flood subsided the
ship lodged against a mountain. As the waters continued to diminish, the
hero sent out successively a dove, a swallow, and finally a raven. The
raven was able to find dry land.]

156. I disembarked [all]; to the four winds I poured a libation.
157. I appointed a sacrifice on the top of the mountain peak;
158. Seven by seven I arranged the sacrificial vessels;
159. Beneath them I piled reeds, cedar wood, and myrtle.
160. The gods smelled the savor,
161. The gods smelled the sweet savor,
162. The gods above the sacrificer collected like flies.[1]

B. Parallel material from Genesis is given for your convenience.

[There is nothing in Genesis about Jahweh's fear facing the vast extent
of the deluge. At the end of the flood Noah sent out first a raven and
then a dove. The dove returned; so Noah waited until upon the third flight
it did not return. Then Noah ventured out.]

8:20,21. Then Noah built an altar to the LORD, and took of every clean
animal and of every clean bird, and offered burnt offerings on the altar.
And when the LORD smelled the pleasing odor, the LORD said in his heart,
"I will never again curse the ground because of man,..."

[1]George A. Barton, *Archaeology and the Bible*, American Sunday-School Union,
Sixth edition, 1933, pp. 335-338.

If you are interested in comparing the human-like language of the Bible with the language found in another early Middle-Eastern account, work through this frame. Since this frame covers an incidental matter you can skip to Frame # 15 without any loss of the logic of the Source Theory.

Frame # 14

Compare the two accounts in the exhibit in order to discover the restraint in the language of the Biblical narrative.

Below two columns are allotted to the accounts labeled "A" and "B" in the exhibit. By placing checks appropriately indicate the application of each statement below. Any statement might apply to *both* accounts.

A   B

___ ___ 1. Birds are sent forth from the ship.

___ ___ 2. A sacrifice is offered, indicating the gratitude of the human beings at their having survived the deluge.

___ ___ 3. The deities are pleased with the smell of the sacrifice.

___ ___ 4. The deities are described as having human reactions in that it is said that they "smelled" the odor.

___ ___ 5. A divine being is described condescendingly in that the deity is compared with a fly.

___ ___ 6. Some restraint is observed in that the pleasure of the divine being is implied but his reaction is not said to be like that of a fly.

ANSWER to Frame # 14

```
A   B

✓   ✓   1. Birds are sent forth from the ship.

✓   ✓   2. A sacrifice is offered, indicating the gratitude of the
           human beings at their having survived the deluge.

✓   ✓   3. The deities are pleased with the smell of the sacrifice.

✓   ✓   4. The deities are described as having human reactions in that
           it is said that they "smelled" the odor.

✓   ___  5. A divine being is described condescendingly in that the
           deity is compared with a fly.

___  ✓   6. Some restraint is observed in that the pleasure of the
           divine being is implied but his reaction is not said to be
           like that of a fly.
```

For some frames now we will concentrate on material from the Jahwist.
Look for the Jahwist's type of language about divine activities.

Genesis 11:1,4-9.	Commentary
Now the whole earth had one language and few words. ...Then they said, "Come, let us build ourselves a city, and a tower with its top in the heavens, and let us make a name for ourselves, lest we be scattered abroad upon the face of the whole earth." And the LORD came down to see the city and the tower, which the sons of men had built. And the LORD said, "Behold, they are one people, and they have all one language; and this is only the beginning of what they will do; and nothing that they propose to do will now be impossible for them. Come, let us go down, and there confuse their language, that they may not understand one another's speech." So the LORD scattered them abroad from there over the face of all the earth, and they left off building the city. Therefore its name was called Babel, because there the LORD confused the language of all the earth; and from there the LORD scattered them abroad over the face of all the earth.	*One language; so everyone understood one another.* *By reason of their unity, men could devise a project.* *Building a tower that would reach to heaven implies that men could then attain divine power.* *The LORD does not wish to share his power with man. Many languages will break up men's unity for they will no longer understand one another.* *By a kind of pun in Hebrew, "Babel," or Babylon, is equated with the word meaning "to confound" or "to mix."*

Underline the elements that complete correctly the following statements.

1. The LORD (came down to see)(saw from heaven) what men were doing with their unity.

2. By implication the story says that the LORD (fears that human beings may lay hold of some of his powers)(understands the good intentions of his human creation).

3. So, according to the story, the LORD (makes it impossible for men to accomplish their dreams)(encourages men by helping them to continue their project).

4. Thus the language used about the deity emphasizes (the intimate and human-like relation of the deity to his human creation)(the remote but kindly nature of the deity).

5. The term used for the deity is a (generic word)(specific name).

ANSWER to Frame # 15

1. The LORD (<u>came down to see</u>)(saw from heaven) what men were doing with their unity.

2. By implication the story says that the LORD (<u>fears that human beings may lay hold of some of his powers</u>)(understands the good intentions of his human creation).

3. So, according to the story, the LORD (<u>makes it impossible for men to accomplish their dreams</u>)(encourages men by helping them to continue their project).

4. Thus the language used about the deity emphasizes (<u>the intimate and human-like relation of the deity to his human creation</u>)(the remote but kindly nature of the deity).

5. The term used for the deity is a (generic word)(<u>specific name</u>).

Instructions for the use of this exhibit are found on the opposite page.

Genesis 11:1,4-9.	Commentary
Now the whole earth had one language and few words. ...Then they said, "Come, let us build ourselves a city, and a tower with its top in the heavens, and <u>let us make a name for ourselves</u>, lest we be scattered abroad upon the face of the whole earth." And the LORD came down to see the city and the tower, which the sons of men had built. And the LORD said, "Behold, they are one people, and they have all one language; and this is only the beginning of what they will do; and nothing that they propose to do will now be impossible for them. Come, let us go down, and <u>there confuse their language, that they may not understand one another's speech</u>." So the LORD scattered them abroad from there over the face of all the earth, and they left off building the city. Therefore its name was called Babel, because there the LORD confused the language of all the earth; and from there the LORD scattered them abroad over the face of all the earth.	*One language; so everyone understood one another.* *By reason of their unity, men could devise a project.* *Building a tower that would reach to heaven implies that men could then attain divine power.* *The LORD does not wish to share his power with man. Many languages will break up men's unity for they will no longer understand one another.* *By a kind of pun in Hebrew, "Babel," or Babylon, is equated with the word meaning "to confound" or "to mix."*

The exhibit for the previous frame has been continued so that you can decide whether the *childlike* elements in the story make the level of reflection *childish*.

The following statements analyze the story in the exhibit for views about the nature of human beings. Place a check before the element that correctly completes each thought.

1. The story implies that the scattering of people comes

   ___ a. merely because man is quarrelsome.

   ___ b. from the inability of men to understand one another [they do not speak the same language].

2. The story says that men were building a tower to the heavens. Ask yourself whether you think the world would be safer if human beings were united and possessed divine powers as well [like possessing the power to accomplish a nuclear reaction?].

   Whatever you think, the Jahwist implies that if men <u>could</u> unite

   ___ a. things would not work out well, for men wish to possess power and fame; the deity suspects that power would not be used by men for the world's good.

   ___ b. they would bring off a constructive project, for men desire the common good above power and fame.

3. Suppose we call *idealistic* a view about man which holds that humans more often than not are working for the good of the world. Then we would term *realistic* a view about man which holds that the good in man often does not prevail over his self-centeredness.

   In terms of such definitions one would classify the Jahwist's views about the nature of man

   ___ a. as idealistic.

   ___ b. as realistic.

4. You have learned something about the depth of reflection in the Jahwist.

   ___ a. If the language about the deity is childlike, the thoughts even about men will be childish.

   ___ b. The language about the deity may be childlike, but the level of reflection is adult.

1. The story implies that the scattering of people comes

   ___ a. merely because man is quarrelsome.

   ✓ b. from the inability of men to understand one another [they do not speak the same language].

2. The story says that men were building a tower to the heavens. Ask yourself whether you think the world would be safer if human beings were united and possessed divine powers as well [like possessing the power to accomplish a nuclear reaction?].

   Whatever you think, the Jahwist implies that if men <u>could</u> unite

   ✓ a. things would not work out well, for men wish to possess power and fame; the deity suspects that power would not be used by men for the world's good.

   ___ b. they would bring off a constructive project, for men desire the common good above power and fame.

3. Suppose we call *idealistic* a view about man which holds that humans more often than not are working for the good of the world. Then we would term *realistic* a view about man which holds that the good in man often does not prevail over his self-centeredness.

   In terms of such definitions one would classify the Jahwist's views about the nature of man

   ___ a. as idealistic.

   ✓ b. as realistic.

4. You have learned something about the depth of reflection in the Jahwist.

   ___ a. If the language about the deity is childlike, the thoughts even about men will be childish.

   ✓ b. The language about the deity may be childlike, but the level of reflection is adult.

Read the story below to note the informality of the relationship between humans and the deity in Jahwist material. Does the deity possess any power?

Genesis 18:1-5,9-15.	Commentary
And the LORD appeared to him by the oaks of Mamre, as he sat at the door of his tent in the heat of the day. He lifted up his eyes and looked, and behold, three men stood in front of him. When he saw them, he ran from the tent door to meet them, and bowed himself to the earth, and said, "My lord, if I have found favor in your sight, do not pass by your servant. Let a little water be brought, and wash your feet, and rest yourselves under the tree, while I fetch a morsel of bread, that you may refresh yourselves, and after that you may pass on--since you have come to your servant." So they said, "Do as you have said." [In verses 6-8 we are told of a very fine meal that Abraham had Sarah prepare for the visitors.] They said to him, "Where is Sarah your wife?" And he [Abraham] said, "She is in the tent." He said, "I will surely return to you in the spring, and Sarah your wife shall have a son." And Sarah was listening at the tent door behind him. Now Abraham and Sarah were old, advanced in age; it had ceased to be with Sarah after the manner of women.	*A puzzling story--it is the LORD who appears in the story, but now Abraham sees three men. Presumably all are divine visitors and the LORD is one of them.* *It is not clear that Abraham knows that one of the three visitors is the LORD, for he receives them as one would any visitors according to the hospitality of the times.* *Perhaps the exceptional extent of the meal is meant to inform the reader that Abraham knows that his visitors are not ordinary humans.* *You will note a curious change from "they" to "he." This source, you see, is not simply the work of one author. This unit you are studying, however, cannot illustrate all the details. For these you need to turn to a standard discussion of the Pentateuch.*

So Sarah laughed to herself, saying, "After I have grown old, and my husband is old, shall I have pleasure?" The LORD said to Abraham, "Why did Sarah laugh, and say, 'Shall I indeed bear a child, now that I am old?' Is anything too hard for the LORD? At the appointed time I will return to you, in the spring, and Sarah shall have a son." But Sarah denied, saying, "I did not laugh"; for she was afraid. He said, "No, but you did laugh."

Underline the elements below that make the statements correct.

1. The deity cannot see Sarah (but in his knowing what she is thinking about his unusual news, the power of the deity is expressed)(and therefore the informality of the relationship between the deity and human beings destroys the presentation of the power of the deity).

2. The LORD knows that this aged couple will have a child (but this is not unusual enough to be an expression of his power)(so the story makes clear that the visitor has unusual powers).

3. Sarah's total reaction to the visitor (shows that she thinks he is just a man, for she laughs)(shows that she recognizes that he is a mysterious figure, for she may laugh but then she is afraid).

1. The deity cannot see Sarah (but in his knowing what she is thinking about his unusual news, the power of the deity is expressed)(and therefore the informality of the relationship between the deity and human beings destroys the presentation of the power of the deity).

2. The LORD knows that this aged couple will have a child (but this is not unusual enough to be an expression of his power)(so the story makes clear that the visitor has unusual powers).

3. Sarah's total reaction to the visitor (shows that she thinks he is just a man, for she laughs)(shows that she recognizes that he is a mysterious figure, for she may laugh but then she is afraid).

Genesis 18:16-28,32-33.= the Jahwist

Then the men set out from there, and
they looked toward Sodom; and Abraham
went with them to set them on their
way. The LORD said, "Shall I hide
from Abraham what I am about to do,
seeing that Abraham shall become a
great and mighty nation, and all
the nations of the earth shall bless
themselves by him? No, for I have
chosen him, that he may charge his
children and his household after him
to keep the way of the LORD by doing
righteousness and justice; so that
the LORD may bring to Abraham what he
has promised him." Then the LORD
said, "Because the outcry against
Sodom and Gomorrah is great and their
sin is very grave, I will go down to
see whether they have done altogether
according to the outcry which has come
to me; and if not, I will know."

        So the men turned from there, and
went toward Sodom; but Abraham still
stood before the LORD. Then Abraham
drew near, and said, "Wilt thou indeed
destroy the righteous with the wicked?
Suppose there are fifty righteous within the city; wilt thou then destroy the
place and not spare it for the fifty
righteous who are in it? Far be it
from thee to do such a thing, to slay
the righteous with the wicked, so that
the righteous fare as the wicked! Far
be that from thee! Shall not the Judge
of all the earth do right?" And the
LORD said, "If I find at Sodom fifty
righteous in the city, I will spare
the whole place for their sake."
Abraham answered, "Behold, I have
taken upon myself to speak to the Lord,
I who am but dust and ashes. Suppose
five of the fifty righteous are lacking? Wilt thou destroy the whole city
for lack of five?" And he said, "I
will not destroy it if I find forty-
five there." [Abraham continues to
bargain for a lower number.]...Then
he [Abraham] said, "Oh let not the
Lord be angry, and I will speak again
but this once. Suppose ten are found
there." He answered, "For the sake of
ten I will not destroy it." And the
LORD went his way,...

Commentary

*This passage immediately follows the
material used in the last frame.*

*Abraham is thought of as more than the
ancestor of Israel.*

*Abraham wishes to make a point with the
LORD because Abraham anticipates that
the LORD will punish Sodom and Gomorrah
if their reputation is deserved.*

*Note that Abraham preserves the bounds
of courteous relationship by using
humble language about himself.*

*Perhaps the story allows the reader to
assume that the LORD knows there are
not even ten righteous people in Sodom.*

Inspect the exhibit on the opposite page to see what the human-like language about the deity makes possible in statements about the divine nature.

Circle the number of the sentences that make *correct* statements about the material in the exhibit.

1. An example of human-like informality in the language about the deity shows up in the fact that Abraham *bargains* with Jahweh over the fate of Sodom and Gomorrah.

2. Another example of informality in the language about the deity appears in the humility that Jahweh shows before Abraham. Jahweh in excessive politeness says that *he is but dust and ashes* in the presence of Abraham.

3. According to the story Jahweh has *come down* to inspect Sodom and Gomorrah, language which implies that otherwise he would not know *all* about what has been going on in these cities.

4. Jahweh informs Abraham about divine intentions about the wicked cities because Jahweh desires to impress Abraham with the might of the deity.

5. Jahweh tells Abraham about the impending visit to the wicked cities because the fate of the wicked may inspire Abraham to guide his children toward a life of undeviating justice.

6. In the human-like language about the deity respect for the difference between Jahweh and man still appears.

7. In the human-like language about the deity, Abraham indicates contempt for the deity.

8. The story shows that Abraham feels that nothing can check the arbitrary power of Jahweh.

9. The story expresses the view that the power of Jahweh is limited by his own just nature.

ANSWER to Frame # 18

1, 3, 5, 6, 9 should be circled.

Genesis 3:22-23.= the *Jahwist*

Then the LORD God said, "Behold, the man has become like one of us, know-ing good and evil; and now, lest he put forth his hand and take also of the tree of life, and eat, and live for ever"--therefore the LORD God sent him forth from the garden of Eden, to till the ground from which he was taken.

Genesis 50:15-17,19,20.= the *Elohist*

When Joseph's brothers saw that their father was dead, they said, "It may be that Joseph will hate us and pay us back for all the evil which we did to him." So they sent a message to Joseph, saying, "Your father gave this command before he died, 'Say to Joseph, Forgive, I pray you, the trans-gression of your brothers and their sin, because they did evil to you.' And now, we pray you, forgive the transgression of the servants of the God of your father." Joseph wept when they spoke to him...Joseph said to them, 'Fear not, for am I in the place of God? As for you, you meant evil against me; but God meant it for good, to bring it about that many people should be kept alive, as they are today."

Material from another source is introduced in the exhibit so that you can judge more precisely the Jahwist's conception of the deity's power.

Place a check before the correct ending of a statement.

1. Jahweh can drive man out of the Garden of Eden without man's permission, but the deity does not know how to cope with man if man eats of the tree of life and lives forever; so in the Jahwist material

    ___ a. the deity is unlimited in his power.

    ___ b. the deity is somewhat limited in his power.

2. The background for Genesis 50 would tell you that Joseph's brothers have done him an injustice [they sold him into slavery, a step which led to Joseph's control over the food resources of the Egyptian kingdom].
    Now the brothers ask Joseph, in the name of the dead father,

    ___ a. to take limited vengeance on them.

    ___ b. to forgive them.

3. Forgiveness of the brothers in the Elohist account

    ___ a. is easy for Joseph. Since Elohim's power is unlimited, the brothers' evil intentions have been used by Elohim for his good purposes. There is thus nothing to forgive.

    ___ b. is difficult for Joseph. Since Elohim's power is limited, nothing can be done about the unending evil that the brothers have started. Thus Joseph's forgiving them would be hypocritical.

4. The Jahwist, in contrast with the Elohist,

    ___ a. continues a tendency already seen--something of a limitation of power in Jahweh.

    ___ b. continues to accent the power of Jahweh even though the language gives Jahweh human emotions.

5. The Elohist, in contrast with the Jahwist,

    ___ a. views the deity's power in the same way, but the terms for the deity are different.

    ___ b. thinks quite differently about the deity's power.

1. Jahweh can drive man out of the Garden of Eden without man's permission, but the deity does not know how to cope with man if man eats of the tree of life and lives forever; so in the Jahwist material

    ___ a. the deity is unlimited in his power.

    ✓ b. the deity is somewhat limited in his power.

2. The background for Genesis 50 would tell you that Joseph's brothers have done him an injustice [they sold him into slavery, a step which led to Joseph's control over the food resources of the Egyptian kingdom].
   Now the brothers ask Joseph, in the name of the dead father,

    ___ a. to take limited vengeance on them.

    ✓ b. to forgive them.

3. Forgiveness of the brothers in the Elohist account

    ✓ a. is easy for Joseph. Since Elohim's power is unlimited, the brothers' evil intentions have been used by Elohim for his good purposes. There is thus nothing to forgive.

    ___ b. is difficult for Joseph. Since Elohim's power is limited, nothing can be done about the unending evil that the brothers have started. Thus Joseph's forgiving them would be hypocritical.

4. The Jahwist, in contrast with the Elohist,

    ✓ a. continues a tendency already seen--something of a limitation of power in Jahweh.

    ___ b. continues to accent the power of Jahweh even though the language gives Jahweh human emotions.

5. The Elohist, in contrast with the Jahwist,

    ___ a. views the deity's power in the same way, but the terms for the deity are different.

    ✓ b. thinks quite differently about the deity's power.

According to the Jahwist, it was Israel's God [Jahweh] who brought about the Creation. But how soon did his human creation recognize God as Jahweh, according to the Jahwist?

Genesis 4:1-2a.

>   Now Adam knew Eve his wife, and she conceived and bore Cain, saying, "I have gotten a man <u>with the help of the LORD</u>." And again, she bore his brother Abel.

Genesis 4:17-22,25,26.

>   Cain knew his wife, and she conceived and bore Enoch; and he built a city, and called the name of the city after the name of his son, Enoch. To Enoch was born Irad; and Irad was the father of Mehujael, and Mehujael the father of Methushael, and Methushael the father of Lamech. And Lamech took two wives; the name of the one was Adah, and the name of the other Zillah. Adah bore Jabal; he was the father of those who dwell in tents and have cattle. His brother's name was Jubal; he was the father of all those who play the lyre and pipe. Zillah bore Tubal-cain; he was the forger of all instruments of bronze and iron. The sister of Tubal-cain was Naamah...And Adam knew his wife again, and she bore a son and called his name Seth, for she said, "God has appointed for me another child instead of Abel, for Cain slew him." <u>To Seth also a son was born, and he called his name Enosh. At that time men began to call upon the name of the LORD.</u>

The births of all the first individuals mentioned have been included in the passages above.

Circle below the number of all sentences that make correct statements about the passages.

1. Eve said that it was by the help of Jahweh she had given birth to Cain.

2. It was not Jahweh but Elohim whom Eve acknowledged as the divine source of her son Cain.

3. By the time of Adam's grandson Enosh, men had begun to worship Jahweh by name.

ANSWER to Frame # 20

---

1 and 3 should be circled.

A. Genesis 18:19,23,25.= the Jahwist

"...I have chosen him, that he may charge his children and his household after him to keep the way of the LORD by doing righteousness and justice; so that the LORD may bring to Abraham what he has promised him."

Then Abraham drew near, and said, "...Far be it from thee to do such a thing, to slay the righteous with the wicked, so that the righteous fare as the wicked! Far be that from thee! Shall not the Judge of all the earth do right?"

B. Exodus 4:24-26.= the Jahwist

At a lodging place on the way the LORD met him and sought to kill him [Moses]. Then Zipporah [Moses' wife] took a flint and cut off her son's foreskin, and touched Moses' feet with it, and said, "Surely you are a bridegroom of blood to me!" So he [Jahweh] let him alone. Then it was that she said, "You are a bridegroom of blood," because of the circumcision.

In "A" [see the exhibit] the Jahwist records the tradition that *the way of Jahweh* requires man to do justice. Another way of saying this—the way of Jahweh requires obedience to ethical rules. [You may wish to review Frame # 18.] "B" introduces the importance of another type of religious rule.

Place a check before the elements that complete correctly the sentences below.

1. According to the story in "B" a certain male had not undergone the ceremony of circumcision. The <u>male in question</u> was

   ___ a. Moses.   ___ b. Moses' son.

2. Moses' wife, alert to the danger, performed the ceremony of circumcision upon

   ___ a. Moses.   ___ b. Moses' son.

The rule regarding circumcision we will call a *ceremonial* [*cultic*] rule. First, distinguish between an ethical and a ceremonial rule, by defining *ethical*.

Definition: Ethical rules promote the well-being of another <u>person</u> or another person's property.
    Examples-- "Do not commit murder."
               "Do not steal."

You can often decide whether a command belongs to the class of the ethical by working out the justification [reasons] for the rule.

3. Take the rule "You shall not commit murder." The justification for this rule lies in the fact that the murderer

   ___ a. would feel strange because he is not conforming to local customs.

   ___ b. damages an individual by taking his life.

Now turn to the *ceremonial*.

Definition: Ceremonial rules guide conduct (a) obedience to which is pleasing to the specific religion or cult; and (b) disobedience to which does not damage [no damage that is obvious at any rate] another person or another person's property.
    Examples-- "You shall make for yourself no molten gods."
               "Every male among you shall be circumcised...He that is eight days old among you shall be circumcised."

4. Take the rule "You shall worship no other god, for the LORD, whose name is Jealous, is a jealous God..." You could <u>reasonably</u> say that the justification of this rule

   ___ a. lies in the fact that disobedience to it damages another person or his property.

   ___ b. lies in the belief of a specific religion that breaking this rule displeases the deity.

1. According to the story in "B" a certain male had not undergone the ceremony of circumcision. The <u>male in question</u> was

   ___ a. Moses.   ✓ b. Moses' son.

2. Moses' wife, alert to the danger, performed the ceremony of circumcision upon

   ___ a. Moses.   ✓ b. Moses' son.

3. Take the rule "You shall not commit murder." The justification for this rule lies in the fact that the murderer

   ___ a. would feel strange because he is not conforming to local customs.

   ✓ b. damages an individual by taking his life.

4. Take the rule "You shall worship no other god, for the LORD, whose name is Jealous, is a jealous God..." You could <u>reasonably</u> say that the justification of this rule

   ___ a. lies in the fact that disobedience to it damages another person or his property.

   ✓ b. lies in the belief of a specific religion that breaking this rule displeases the deity.

This frame will give you practice in working out probable justifications for two of the Jahwist's commandments.

Exodus 34:17,18.

You shall make for yourself no molten gods.

The feast of unleavened bread you shall keep. Seven days you shall eat unleavened bread, as I commanded you, at the time appointed in the month Abib; for in the month Abib you came out from Egypt.

Below are given justifications for the two commandments above. Eliminate the improbable justifications by crossing out the appropriate number.

1. The reason why making molten gods is forbidden lies in the burden that the men would have to assume in transporting heavy gods.

2. The reason for rejecting molten gods lies in the fact that this religion does not accept images.

3. The eating of unleavened bread (bread without yeast in it) is said to commemorate Israel's escape from Egypt, a sacred memory.

4. Israel must eat unleavened bread because the bakers of Israel need a rest.

ANSWER to Frame # 22

1 and 4 are improbable.

Remember that we are working out a flat distinction.
[*Don't make your task difficult* by reflecting that in life distinctions between
ethical and ceremonial rules become confusing because human beings offer
varying justifications for their conduct.]

Below are found the Jahwist's Ten Commandments.* [Exodus 34:14,17-23,25,26.]

I. Circle the number of any commandment that is *ceremonial*, using the definitions in Frame # 21.

   1. ...you shall worship no other god, for the LORD, whose name is Jealous,
      is a jealous God...

   2. You shall make for yourself no molten gods.

   3. The feast of unleavened bread you shall keep. Seven days you shall eat
      unleavened bread, as I commanded you, at the time appointed in the
      month Abib; for in the month Abib you came out from Egypt.

   4. All that opens the womb is mine, all your male cattle, the firstlings of
      cow and sheep. The firstling of an ass you shall redeem with a lamb, or
      if you will not redeem it you shall break its neck. All the first-born
      of your sons you shall redeem. And none shall appear before me empty.

   5. Six days you shall work, but on the seventh day you shall rest; in
      plowing time and in harvest you shall rest.

   6. And you shall observe the feast of weeks, the first fruits of wheat har-
      vest, and the feast of ingathering at the year's end. Three times in
      the year shall all your males appear before the LORD God, the God of
      Israel.

   7. You shall not offer the blood of my sacrifice with leaven [yeast];

   8. Neither shall the sacrifice of the feast of the passover be left until
      the morning.

   9. The first of the first fruits of your ground you shall bring to the
      house of the LORD your God.

   10. You shall not boil a kid [goat] in its mother's milk.

II. Circle the number of the statement below that offers the correct generali-
    zation about the number of ceremonial commands in the Jahwist's Ten
    Commandments.

    11. All the Jahwist's Ten Commandments are ceremonial.

    12. Some of the Jahwist's Ten Commandments are ceremonial. Some are not.

* *The next frame offers the reasons for calling this set a Ten Commandments.
  If you are not curious about the matter you may wish to skip Frame # 24.*

I. Circle the number of any commandment that is *ceremonial*, using the definitions in Frame # 21.

①. ...you shall worship no other god, for the LORD, whose name is Jealous, is a jealous God...

②. You shall make for yourself no molten gods.

③. The feast of unleavened bread you shall keep. Seven days you shall eat unleavened bread, as I commanded you, at the time appointed in the month Abib; for in the month Abib you came out from Egypt.

④. All that opens the womb is mine, all your male cattle, the firstlings of cow and sheep. The firstling of an ass you shall redeem with a lamb, or if you will not redeem it you shall break its neck. All the first-born of your sons you shall redeem. And none shall appear before me empty.

⑤. Six days you shall work, but on the seventh day you shall rest; in plowing time and in harvest you shall rest.

⑥. And you shall observe the feast of weeks, the first fruits of wheat harvest, and the feast of ingathering at the year's end. Three times in the year shall all your males appear before the LORD God, the God of Israel.

⑦. You shall not offer the blood of my sacrifice with leaven [yeast];

⑧. Neither shall the sacrifice of the feast of the passover be left until the morning.

⑨. The first of the first fruits of your ground you shall bring to the house of the LORD your God.

⑩. You shall not boil a kid [goat] in its mother's milk.

II. Circle the number of the statement below that offers the correct generalization about the number of ceremonial commands in the Jahwist's Ten Commandments.

⑪. All the Jahwist's Ten Commandments are ceremonial.

12. Some of the Jahwist's Ten Commandments are ceremonial. Some are not.

The quotation below from Exodus immediately precedes the commandments given in the last frame.
Look for proof that a version of the Ten Commandments is to follow.

Exodus 34:1,2,4-6,10,11.

The LORD said to Moses, "Cut two tables of stone <u>like the first</u>; and I will write upon the tables the words that were on the first tables, which you broke. Be ready in the morning, and come up in the morning to Mount Sinai, and present yourself there to me on the top of the mountain... So Moses cut two tables of stone <u>like the first</u>; and he rose early in the morning and went up on Mount Sinai, as the LORD had commanded him, and took in his hand two tables of stone. And the LORD descended in the cloud and stood with him there, and proclaimed the name of the LORD. The LORD passed before him, and proclaimed, "The LORD, the LORD, a God merciful and gracious, slow to anger, and abounding in steadfast love and faithfulness,...
And he said, "Behold, I make a covenant... Observe what I command you this day..."

Preceding the passage above, the tradition has been recorded that Jahweh's commandments have been written on tablets of stone. Moses had stayed so long on the mountain, however, that the people had turned to the worship of a calf cast in metal. When Moses came down from the mountain he was so shocked by the worship of the golden calf that he threw down the stone tablets.

Circle the numbers below of more probable interpretations of the passage above.

1. Since Jahweh points out that Moses has broken the commandments, the words which are to follow will be very different from the ones that were first given.

2. Since Jahweh is going to write "the words that were on the first tables," the words now being given will be repetitions.

3. When it is said that Moses has broken something, the meaning is that Moses has broken the tablets; it does not mean that he has broken Jahweh's commands.

4. The commands that are to follow constitute a "covenant" [a compact].

ANSWER to Frame # 24

2, 3, and 4 should be circled.

Exodus 34:14,17-23,25,26.= Jahwist	**Exodus 20:3,4,7-10,12-17.= Elohist**

...you shall worship no other god,...

You shall make for yourself no molten gods.

The feast of unleavened bread you shall keep. Seven days you shall eat unleavened bread, as I commanded you, at the time appointed in the month Abib;...
  All that opens the womb is mine, all your male cattle, the first-lings of cow and sheep. The first-ling of an ass you shall redeem with a lamb, or if you will not re-deem it you shall break its neck. All the first-born of your sons you shall redeem. And none shall ap-pear before me empty.

Six days you shall work, but on the seventh day you shall rest; in plow-ing time and in harvest you shall rest.

And you shall observe the feast of weeks, the first fruits of wheat har-vest, and the feast of ingathering at the year's end. Three times in the year shall all your males appear be-fore the LORD God, the God of Israel...
  You shall not offer the blood of my sacrifice with leaven;
neither shall the sacrifice of the feast of the passover be left until the morning.
  The first of the first fruits of your ground you shall bring to the house of the LORD your God.
You shall not boil a kid in its mother's milk.

1. You shall have no other gods before me.
2. You shall not make yourself a graven image, or any likeness of anything...

3. You shall not take the name of the LORD your God in vain; for the LORD will not hold him guiltless who takes his name in vain.
    4. Remember the sabbath day, to keep it holy. Six days you shall labor, and do all your work; but the seventh day is a sabbath to the LORD your God;...

5. Honor your father and your mother,...
    6. You shall not kill.
7. You shall not commit adultery.
    8. You shall not steal.
9. You shall not bear false witness against your neighbor.
    10. You shall not covet...anything that is your neighbor's.

To reinforce your grasp of the Jahwist's interest in the ceremonial, the exhibit gives you both his and the Elohist's sets of Ten Commandments arranged so that the Commandments common to both can be identified easily.
Examine the two columns to evaluate the relative importance of the ceremonial and the ethical respectively.

1. Set down which of the Jahwist's Ten Commandments involves an injury done to another person or another person's property.

   _____
   _____
   _____
   _____
   _____

2. Set down which of the Elohist's Ten Commandments involves an injury done to another person or another person's property.

   _____
   _____
   _____
   _____
   _____

3. The Jahwist's interest in the ceremonial aspects of religion, including all the Jahwist's material examined so far,

   ____ a. has excluded the ethical, for just as in the story of Abraham's bargaining with Jahweh over the fate of Sodom, so here any demand for ethical behavior is lacking.

   ____ b. is very strong although one would argue on the basis of the story about Abraham's bargaining with Jahweh over the fate of Sodom that there is some interest in the ethical as well.

4. Considering both ethical and ceremonial commandments and comparing with the Jahwist's set of commandments, the interest of the Elohist lies

   ____ a. both in the ceremonial and ethical, unlike the Jahwist's set.

   ____ b. only in the ceremonial, unlike the Jahwist's set.

1. Set down which of the Jahwist's Ten Commandments involves an injury done to another person or another person's property.

   Most students indicate correctly that none of the Jahwist's Ten Commandments involves an injury done either to another person or to another person's property.

2. Set down which of the Elohist's Ten Commandments involves an injury done to another person or another person's property.

   Some of the Elohist's commandments very clearly involve injury to another person:

   You shall not kill (another's life)
   You shall not commit adultery (psychic damage to the husband or wife)
   You shall not steal (depriving another of his property)
   You shall not bear false witness (damage at least to the reputation of another)

   One commandment implies the possibility of damaging another:
   You shall not covet (a most unusual commandment because it speaks about an attitude rather than an act--an attitude that could motivate one to do injury to another person)

   One commandment received divided judgements--Honor thy father and thy mother. (For various reasons some consider this a ceremonial commandment, and others think of it as an ethical commandment.)

3. The Jahwist's interest in the ceremonial aspects of religion, including all the Jahwist's material examined so far,

   ___ a. has excluded the ethical, for just as in the story of Abraham's bargaining with Jahweh over the fate of Sodom, so here any demand for ethical behavior is lacking.

   ✓ b. is very strong although one would argue on the basis of the story about Abraham's bargaining with Jahweh over the fate of Sodom that there is some interest in the ethical as well.

4. Considering both ethical and ceremonial commandments and comparing with the Jahwist's set of commandments, the interest of the Elohist lies

   ✓ a. both in the ceremonial and ethical, unlike the Jahwist's set.

   ___ b. only in the ceremonial, unlike the Jahwist's set.

Genesis 12:10-20.= Jahwist

Now there was a famine in the land. So Abram went down to Egypt to sojourn there, for the famine was severe in the land. When he was about to enter Egypt, he said to Sarai his wife, "I know that you are a woman beautiful to behold; and when the Egyptians see you, they will say, 'This is his wife'; then they will kill me, but they will let you live. Say you are my sister, that it may go well with me because of you, and that my life may be spared on your account." When Abram entered Egypt the Egyptians saw that the woman was very beautiful. And when the princes of Pharaoh saw her, they praised her to Pharaoh. And the woman was taken into Pharaoh's house. And for her sake he dealt well with Abram; and he had sheep, oxen, he-asses, menservants, maidservants, she-asses, and camels.
But the LORD afflicted Pharaoh and his house with great plagues because of Sarai, Abram's wife. So Pharaoh called Abram, and said, "What is this you have done to me? Why did you not tell me that she was your wife? <u>Why did you say, 'She is my sister,'</u> so that I took her for my wife? Now then, here is your wife, take her, and be gone." And Pharoah gave men orders concerning him; and they set him on the way, with his wife and all that he had.

Genesis 20:1-13.= Elohist

From there Abraham journeyed toward the territory of the Negeb, and dwelt between Kadesh and Shur; and he sojourned in Gerar. And <u>Abraham said of Sarah his wife, "She is my sister."</u> And Abimelech king of Gerar sent and took Sarah. But God came to Abimelech in a dream by night, and said to him, "Behold, you are a dead man, because of the woman whom you have taken; for she is a man's wife." Now Abimelech had not approached her; so he said, "Lord, wilt thou slay an innocent people? Did he not himself say to me, 'She is my sister'? And she herself said, 'He is my brother.' In the integrity of my heart and the innocence of my hands I have done this." Then God said to him in the dream, "Yes, I know that you have done this in the integrity of your heart, and it was I who kept you from sinning against me; therefore I did not let you touch her. Now then restore the man's wife; for he is a prophet, and he will pray for you, and you shall live. But if you do not restore her, know that you shall surely die, you, and all that are yours."
So Abimelech rose early in the morning, and called all his servants, and told them all these things; and the men were very much afraid. Then Abimelech called Abraham, and said to him, "What have you done to us? And how have I sinned against you, that you have brought on me and my kingdom a great sin? You have done to me things that ought not to be done." And Abimelech said to Abraham, <u>"What were you thinking of, that you did this thing?"</u> Abraham said, "I did it because I thought, There is no fear of God at all in this place, and they will kill me because of my wife. <u>Besides she is indeed my sister, the daughter of my father but not the daughter of my mother</u>; and she became my wife. And when God caused me to wander from my father's house, I said to her, 'This is the kindness you must do me; at every place to which we come, say of me, He is my brother.'"

Is the Jahwist interested in giving ethical motivations to the heroes of Israel?

Compare the two stories in the exhibit and see at what points there are differences.

Note: One tradition called an Israelite hero and his wife "Abram and Sarai;" another called the same people "Abraham and Sarah."

Circle the numbers of the <u>correct</u> statements.

1. In the Jahwist's story, in the Hebrew the name "Jahweh" appears, but in the other story the generic term "Elohim" is used.

2. In both stories Abraham says that his wife is his sister.

3. In both stories it is pointed out that Sarah really is Abraham's sister --that is, she is his half-sister.

4. In the Jahwist story, nothing is said afterwards about Sarah's being Abraham's real sister; so we can assume that there is no worry about Abraham's having told a lie.

5. The Jahwist is not content with the possibility that the reader might think of Abraham as a coward and a liar; thus he makes it clear that Abraham was not telling a lie, and that it was a manly thing to do to pass Sarah off as his sister since there were non-believers around.

ANSWER to Frame # 26

1, 2, and 4 are correct.

Genesis 16:1-6.

Now Sarai, Abram's wife, bore him no
children. She had an Egyptian maid
whose name was Hagar; and Sarai said
to Abram, "Behold now, the LORD has
prevented me from bearing children;
go in to my maid; it may be that I
shall obtain children by her." And
Abram hearkened to the voice of Sarai.
So, after Abram had dwelt ten years
in the land of Canaan, Sarai, Abram's
wife, took Hagar the Egyptian her maid,
and gave her to Abram her husband as a
wife. And he went in to Hagar, and she
conceived; and when she saw that she
had conceived, she looked with contempt
on her mistress. And Sarai said to
Abram, "May the wrong done to me be on
you! I gave my maid to your embrace,
and when she saw that she had conceived,
she looked on me with contempt. May
the LORD judge between you and me!"
But Abram said to Sarai, "Behold, your
maid is in your power; <u>do to her as you
please</u>." Then Sarai dealt harshly with
her, and she fled from her.

Genesis 21:2,3,8-14.

And Sarah conceived, and bore Abraham a
son in his old age at the time of which
God had spoken to him. Abraham called
the name of his son who was born to him,
whom Sarah bore him, Isaac....
And the child grew, and was weaned;
and Abraham made a great feast on the
day that Isaac was weaned. But Sarah
saw the son of Hagar the Egyptian, whom
she had borne to Abraham, playing with
her son Isaac. So she said to Abraham,
"Cast out this slave woman with her
son; for the son of this slave woman
shall not be heir with my son Isaac."
<u>And the thing was very displeasing to
Abraham on account of his son</u>. But
God said to Abraham, "Be not displeased
because of the lad and because of your
slave woman; whatever Sarah says to
you, do as she tells you, for through
Isaac shall your descendants be named.
And I will make a nation of the son of
the slave woman also, because he is
your offspring." So Abraham rose early in the morning, and took bread and
a skin of water, and gave it to Hagar,
putting it on her shoulder, along with
the child, and sent her away. And she
departed, and wandered in the wilderness of Beer-sheba.

Test your knowledge of the characteristics of the Jahwist strand of material by answering the questions below.

1. Which column contains the Jahwist material? _____

2. State in detail why you chose the specific column.

   A. What is the term for the deity? _____

   _____

   B. In both columns Abraham has a child by his wife's servant. How does he react to Sarah's treatment of the servant and the servant's child?

   _____

   _____

   _____

   _____

   _____

   _____

   _____

   C. Any other evidence that helped you to distinguish which column belongs to the Jahwist?

   _____

   _____

   _____

   _____

1. Which column contains the Jahwist material? *Left-hand.*

2. State in detail why you chose the specific column. *Student answers have run something like the following:*

   A. What is the term for the deity? *The left-hand column uses the specific term, Jahweh, while the right-hand column uses the generic, Elohim. [If you missed this easily observed fact, you should go back and drill on Frames # 7 and # 8.]*

   B. In both columns Abraham has a child by his wife's servant. How does he react to Sarah's treatment of the servant and the servant's child?

      The left-hand column displays Abraham as unconcerned about the fate of Hagar when he faced the jealousy of Sarah. The right-hand column says that Abraham was displeased with Sarah's rejection of her rival and did what he could to make Hagar's journey more bearable. The willingness to allow Abraham to appear with human weaknesses resembles the previous passage from the Jahwist's material. [If you missed this more difficult matter, review Frame # 26.]

   C. Any other evidence that helped you to distinguish which column belongs to the Jahwist?

      The terms "Abram and Sarai" were characteristic of the Jahwist in Frame # 26. [Since this is a minor characteristic, don't worry if you missed it.]

Two common <u>mistakes</u>: If you have either of the following, you are making distinctions for which the specific passages provide <u>no</u> example.

1. You try to find illustrations of the Jahwist's interest in ceremonial rules. *[Perhaps you need to go back to Frame # 21 to note that the Jahwist's interest has to do with ceremonial rules which are at the same time <u>religious</u> rules. Many ceremonies exist in a culture that may not belong to a religion, by the way.]*

2. You try to find an illustration of an ethical interest in the Jahwist material because in Frame # 18 Abraham insists that "the Judge of all the earth do right." *[In general, it is sensible to realize that no author or tradition works <u>every</u> special point of view into any given passage.]*

Genesis 16:1-6 the Schemer

Now Sarai, Abram's wife, bore him no
children. She had an Egyptian maid
whose name was Hagar; and Sarai said
to Abram, "Behold now, the LORD has
prevented me from bearing children;
go in to my maid; it may be that I
shall obtain children by her." And
Abram hearkened to the voice of Sarai.
So, after Abram had dwelt ten years
in the land of Canaan, Sarai, Abram's
wife, took Hagar the Egyptian her maid,
and gave her to Abram her husband as a
wife. And he went in to Hagar, and she
conceived; and when she saw that she
had conceived, she looked with contempt
on her mistress. And Sarai said to
Abram, "May the wrong done to me be on
you! I gave my maid to your embrace,
and when she saw that she had conceived,
she looked on me with contempt. May
the LORD judge between you and me!"
But Abram said to Sarai, "Behold, your
maid is in your power; do to her as you
please." Then Sarai dealt harshly with
her, and she fled from her.

Genesis 21:x, 9.8-14.- the Mother

And Sarah conceived, and bore Abraham a
son in his old age at the time of which
God had spoken to him. Abraham called
the name of his son who was born to him,
whom Sarah bore him, Isaac....
And the child grew, and was weaned;
and Abraham made a great feast on the
day that Isaac was weaned. But Sarah
saw the son of Hagar the Egyptian, whom
she had borne to Abraham, playing with
her son Isaac. So she said to Abraham,
"Cast out this slave woman with her
son; for the son of this slave woman
shall not be heir with my son Isaac."
And the thing was very displeasing to
Abraham on account of his son. But
God said to Abraham, "Be not displeased
because of the lad and because of your
slave woman; whatever Sarah says to
you, do as she tells you, for through
Isaac shall your descendants be named.
And I will make a nation of the son of
the slave woman also, because he is
your offspring." So Abraham rose early
in the morning, and took bread and a
skin of water, and gave it to Hagar,
putting it on her shoulder, along with
the child, and sent her away. And she
departed, and wandered in the wilderness
of Beer-sheba.

Genesis 16:1-6.= the Jahwist	Genesis 21:2,3,8-14.= the Elohist
Now Sarai, Abram's wife, bore him no children. She had an Egyptian maid whose name was Hagar; and Sarai said to Abram, "Behold now, the LORD has prevented me from bearing children; go in to my maid; it may be that I shall obtain children by her." And Abram hearkened to the voice of Sarai. So, after Abram had dwelt ten years in the land of Canaan, Sarai, Abram's wife, took Hagar the Egyptian her maid, and gave her to Abram her husband as a wife. And he went in to Hagar, and she conceived; and when she saw that she had conceived, she looked with contempt on her mistress. And Sarai said to Abram, "May the wrong done to me be on you! I gave my maid to your embrace, and when she saw that she had conceived, she looked on me with contempt. May the LORD judge between you and me!" But Abram said to Sarai, "Behold, your maid is in your power; do to her as you please." Then Sarai dealt harshly with her, and she fled from her.	And Sarah conceived, and bore Abraham a son in his old age at the time of which God had spoken to him. Abraham called the name of his son who was born to him, whom Sarah bore him, Isaac.... And the child grew, and was weaned; and Abraham made a great feast on the day that Isaac was weaned. But Sarah saw the son of Hagar the Egyptian, whom she had borne to Abraham, playing with her son Isaac. So she said to Abraham, "Cast out this slave woman with her son; for the son of this slave woman shall not be heir with my son Isaac." And the thing was very displeasing to Abraham on account of his son. But God said to Abraham, "Be not displeased because of the lad and because of your slave woman; whatever Sarah says to you, do as she tells you, for through Isaac shall your descendants be named. And I will make a nation of the son of the slave woman also, because he is your offspring." So Abraham rose early in the morning, and took bread and a skin of water, and gave it to Hagar, putting it on her shoulder, along with the child, and sent her away. And she departed, and wandered in the wilderness of Beer-sheba.

The exhibit from the previous frame has been repeated so that you can study the right-hand column as representative of the source called the *Elohist*.

Underline the elements that make the following sentences correct.

1. The Elohist uses in *Genesis* (the specific name of a deity "Jahweh") (the generic term "Elohim").

2. Judging by his portrayal of Abraham in this story, the Elohist prefers that the heroes of Israel be (as humane as possible)(rather callous masculine figures).

ANSWER to Frame # 28

1. The Elohist used in *Genesis* (the specific name of a deity "Jahweh") (<u>the generic term "Elohim"</u>).

2. Judging by his portrayal of Abraham in this story, the Elohist prefers that the heroes of Israel be (<u>as humane as possible</u>)(rather callous masculine figures).

A. Genesis 1:1-3.= Priestly

In the beginning God created the heavens and the earth. The earth was without form and void, and darkness was upon the face of the deep; and the Spirit of God was moving over the face of the waters. And God said, "Let there be light"; and there was light.

B. Leviticus 19:1-3.= Priestly

And the LORD said to Moses, "Say to all the congregation of the people of Israel, You shall be holy; for I the LORD your God am holy. Every one of you shall revere his mother and his father, and you shall keep my sabbaths..."

C. Genesis 2:4b,5.= Jahwist

In the day that the LORD God made the earth and the heavens, when no plant of the field was yet in the earth and no herb of the field had yet sprung up--for the LORD God had not caused it to rain upon the earth, and there was no man to till the ground...

D. Exodus 34:1,26.= Jahwist

The LORD said to Moses, "Cut two tables of stone like the first; and I will write upon the tables the words that were on the first tables, which you broke."
"The first of the first fruits of your ground you shall bring to the house of the LORD your God. You shall not boil a kid in its mother's milk."

E. Genesis 20:1-3.= Elohist

From there Abraham journeyed toward the territory of the Negeb, and dwelt between Kadesh and Shur; and he sojourned in Gerar. And Abraham said of Sarah his wife, "She is my sister." And Abimelech king of Gerar sent and took Sarah. But God came to Abimelech in a dream by night, and said to him, "Behold, you are a dead man, because of the woman whom you have taken; for she is a man's wife."

F. Exodus 20:1-3,12,13.= Elohist

And God spoke all these words, saying, "I am the LORD your God, who brought you out of the land of Egypt, out of the house of bondage. You shall have no other gods before me."
"Honor your father and your mother, that your days may be long in the land which the LORD your God gives you. You shall not kill."

The use of the generic term *Jahweh* has been employed to identify the Jahwist. But you need to know now that the identification of the different sources is complicated. Inspect the samples of three different sources in the exhibit for the terms used for the deity.

Circle the <u>letters</u> of conclusions that are valid. Note that in some cases more than one conclusion fits the evidence.

1. The term *Jahweh*

    a. is used only by the Jahwist.
    b. appears at some time in all three sources.

2. The term *Elohim*

    a. is not used by the Jahwist without the term *Jahweh* nearby.
    b. appears alone <u>in Genesis</u> in both the Priestly and the Elohist sources.
    c. combined with *Jahweh*, or at any rate in the same sentence with *Jahweh*, appears outside of Genesis in both the Priestly and Elohist sources.
    d. is used <u>without</u> *Jahweh* in all passages belonging to both the Priestly and the Elohist sources.

3. Since the Elohist has left no creation story for us

    a. the use of *Jahweh* in "C" identifies that Creation story as Jahwist, for the Priestly source uses *Elohim* in his Creation story.
    b. it is impossible to tell by the use of the term for the deity whether "C" is either Jahwist or Priestly.

4. If you forget that <u>the Elohist left no creation story</u>

    a. you still would not call "A" Elohist because *Elohim* appears in "A."
    b. you could make the mistake of calling "A" the work of the Elohist.

5. If you forget that outside of Genesis the Elohist can use *Jahweh*

    a. you still would not call "F" Jahwist because the Jahwist's Ten Commandments contain no ethical rules.
    b. you could make the mistake of calling "F" Jahwist.

6. Since later you will learn that <u>all of Leviticus is Priestly</u>

    a. you still need to be confused by the fact that the Priestly source uses *Jahweh* in "B."
    b. no reason for confusion will exist with the examination of "B" so long as you remember that <u>in Genesis only</u> the Priestly source confines itself to *Elohim* generally.

ANSWER to Frame # 29

1. The term *Jahweh*

    a. is used only by the Jahwist.
    ⓑ. appears at some time in all three sources.

2. The term *Elohim*

    ⓐ. is not used by the Jahwist without the term *Jahweh* nearby.
    ⓑ. appears alone <u>in Genesis</u> in both the Priestly and the Elohist sources.
    ⓒ. combined with *Jahweh*, or at any rate in the same sentence with *Jahweh*, appears outside of Genesis in both the Priestly and Elohist sources.
    d. is used <u>without</u> *Jahweh* in all passages belonging to both the Priestly and the Elohist sources.

3. Since the Elohist has left no creation story for us

    ⓐ. the use of *Jahweh* in "C" identifies that Creation story as Jahwist, for the Priestly source uses *Elohim* in his Creation story.
    b. it is impossible to tell by the use of the term for the deity whether "C" is either Jahwist or Priestly.

4. If you forget that <u>the Elohist left no creation story</u>

    a. you still would not call "A" Elohist because *Elohim* appears in "A."
    ⓑ. you could make the mistake of calling "A" the work of the Elohist.

5. If you forget that outside of Genesis the Elohist can use *Jahweh*

    ⓐ. you still would not call "F" Jahwist because the Jahwist's Ten Commandments contain no ethical rules.
    b. you could make the mistake of calling "F" Jahwist.

6. Since later you will learn that <u>all of Leviticus is Priestly</u>

    a. you still need to be confused by the fact that the Priestly source uses *Jahweh* in "B."
    ⓑ. no reason for confusion will exist with the examination of "B" so long as you remember that <u>in Genesis only</u> the Priestly source confines itself to *Elohim* generally.

Exodus 3:13-15.= Elohist

Then Moses said to God, "If I come to the people of Israel and say to them, 'The God of your fathers has sent me to you,' and they ask me, 'What is his name?' what shall I say to them?" God said to Moses, "I AM WHO I AM."... God also said to Moses, "Say this to the people of Israel, 'The LORD, the God of your fathers, the God of Abraham, the God of Isaac, and the God of Jacob, has sent me to you': this is my name for ever, and thus I am to be remembered throughout all generations."

Commentary

Moses has been commissioned to lead his people out of slavery to the Egyptians. He is doubtful that his people will accept him as a leader; so he feels he needs special information--what is the name of the Elohim who is commissioning him?

In Hebrew thought the name _is_ the identity of a person; the name is not simply an arbitrary arrangement of sounds or of letters. To ask for Elohim's name therefore is to ask for the identity of the God.

In the Elohist's answer, the name Jahweh is explained as arising from the verb "to be." Hence "I am who I am." Another way of saying it: "BEING that is everlasting." "The same BEING yesterday, today, and forever." A marginal note in the translation used in this program: "I WILL BE WHAT I WILL BE."

Genesis 4:17-22,25,26.= Jahwist

Cain knew his wife, and she conceived and bore Enoch; and he built a city, and called the name of the city after the name of his son, Enoch. To Enoch was born Irad; and Irad was the father of Mehujael, and Mehujael the father of Methushael, and Methushael the father of Lamech. And Lamech took two wives; the name of the one was Adah, and the name of the other Zillah. Adah bore Jabal; he was the father of those who dwell in tents and have cattle. His brother's name was Jubal; he was the father of all those who play the lyre and pipe. Zillah bore Tubal-cain; he was the forger of all instruments of bronze and iron. The sister of Tubal-cain was Naamah...And Adam knew his wife again, and she bore a son and called his name Seth, for she said, "God has appointed for me another child instead of Abel, for Cain slew him." To Seth also a son was born, and he called his name Enosh. At that time men began to call upon the name of the LORD.

By this time you have learned that in Genesis only does the Elohist use Elohim exclusively. The Elohist has a special theory about the time when Israel came to know Elohim's true identity; i.e., Jahweh. [The passage in the lower part of the exhibit is repeated from Frame # 20 to remind you of the Jahwist's theory about how early Jahweh was known by name.]

Place a check before the correct conclusions.

Review the Jahwist's theory.

1. The Jahwist believes that Jahweh was the Creator,

   ___ a. but not until Abraham did men come to know Elohim as Jahweh.

   ___ b. and as early as Adam's grandson men called upon the name of Jahweh.

Now as to the Elohist's special theory.

2. According to the first line of the exhibit, Moses addresses the deity

   ___ a. as Elohim.

   ___ b. as Jahweh.

3. The deity tells Moses that the Elohim of Abraham, Isaac, and Jacob is

   ___ a. Elohim.

   ___ b. Jahweh.

4. There are two theories that are being expressed in the passage in the exhibit: the name Jahweh is said to mean "I AM WHO I AM;" and

   ___ a. Elohim's true nature was revealed to Moses so that he could inform Israel.

   ___ b. Jahweh's true name as Elohim must be remembered from generation to generation.

5. From the time of Moses on, it will not be surprising if the Elohist uses as the term for the deity

   ___ a. Elohim.

   ___ b. Jahweh.

1. The Jahwist believes that Jahweh was the Creator,

   ___ a. but not until Abraham did men come to know Elohim as Jahweh.

   ✓ b. and as early as Adam's grandson men called upon the name of Jahweh. *If you missed this, review Frame # 20.*

2. According to the first line of the exhibit, Moses addresses the deity

   ✓ a. as Elohim.

   ___ b. as Jahweh.

3. The deity tells Moses that the Elohim of Abraham, Isaac, and Jacob is

   ___ a. Elohim.

   ✓ b. Jahweh.

4. There are two theories that are being expressed in the passage in the exhibit: the name Jahweh is said to mean "I AM WHO I AM;" and

   ✓ a. Elohim's true nature was revealed to Moses so that he could inform Israel.

   ___ b. Jahweh's true name as Elohim must be remembered from generation to generation.

5. From the time of Moses on, it will not be surprising if the Elohist uses as the term for the deity

   ___ a. Elohim.

   ✓ b. Jahweh.

Genesis 12:10-20.= Jahwist	Genesis 20:1-13.= Elohist
Now there was a famine in the land. So Abram went down to Egypt to sojourn there, for the famine was severe in the land. When he was about to enter Egypt, he said to Sarai his wife, "I know that you are a woman beautiful to behold; and when the Egyptians see you, they will say, 'This is his wife'; then they will kill me, but they will let you live. Say you are my sister, that it may go well with me because of you, and that my life may be spared on your account." When Abram entered Egypt the Egyptians saw that the woman was very beautiful. And when the princes of Pharaoh saw her, they praised her to Pharaoh. And the woman was taken into Pharaoh's house. And for her sake he dealt well with Abram; and he had sheep, oxen, he-asses, menservants, maidservants, she-asses, and camels. But the LORD afflicted Pharaoh and his house with great plagues because of Sarai, Abram's wife. So Pharaoh called Abram, and said, "What is this you have done to me? Why did you not tell me that she was your wife? Why did you say, 'She is my sister,' so that I took her for my wife? Now then, here is your wife, take her, and be gone." And Pharaoh gave men orders concerning him; and they set him on the way, with his wife and all that he had.	From there Abraham journeyed toward the territory of the Negeb, and dwelt between Kadesh and Shur; and he sojourned in Gerar. And Abraham said of Sarah his wife, "She is my sister." And Abimelech king of Gerar sent and took Sarah. But God came to Abimelech in a dream by night, and said to him, "Behold, you are a dead man, because of the woman whom you have taken; for she is a man's wife." Now Abimelech had not approached her; so he said, "Lord, wilt thou slay an innocent people? Did he not himself say to me, 'She is my sister'? And she herself said, 'He is my brother.' In the integrity of my heart and the innocence of my hands I have done this." Then God said to him in the dream, "Yes, I know that you have done this in the integrity of your heart, and it was I who kept you from sinning against me; therefore I did not let you touch her. Now then restore the man's wife; for he is a prophet, and he will pray for you, and you shall live. But if you do not restore her, know that you shall surely die, you, and all that are yours." So Abimelech rose early in the morning, and called all his servants, and told them all these things; and the men were very much afraid. Then Abimelech called Abraham, and said to him, "What have you done to us? And how have I sinned against you, that you have brought on me and my kingdom a great sin? You have done to me things that ought not to be done." And Abimelech said to Abraham, "What were you thinking of, that you did this thing?" Abraham said, "I did it because I thought, There is no fear of God at all in this place, and they will kill me because of my wife. Besides she is indeed my sister, the daughter of my father but not the daughter of my mother; and she became my wife. And

when God caused me to wander from my father's house, I said to her, 'This is
the kindness you must do me; at every place to which we come, say of me, He is
my brother.'"

The exhibit from Frame # 26 has been repeated so that you may continue to study the characteristics of the Elohist.

Circle the numbers of all correct statements below.

1. Abimelech says to God [12th and 13th lines from the top]: "Lord, wilt thou slay an innocent people?" The use of the term "Lord" shows that the Elohist is inconsistent, for in *Genesis* he is using "Jahweh."

2. The term for the deity is used consistently, for in *Genesis* the Elohist restricts himself generally to the generic term for the deity.

3. The emphasis in the story upon a dream as the means of communication between God and Abimelech shows that the Elohist, unlike the Jahwist, prefers not to show the deity as appearing in a human shape.

4. The Elohist is consistent with the material in Frame # 28 by portraying Abraham as more ethical in contrast to the Jahwist's material.

ANSWER to Frame # 31

2, 3, and 4 are correct statements.

Genesis 20:3-6.

But God came to Abimelech in a dream by night, and said to him, "Behold, you are
a dead man, because of the woman whom you have taken; for she is a man's wife."
Now Abimelech had not approached her; so he said, "Lord, wilt thou slay an innocent people? Did he not himself say to me, 'She is my sister'? And she herself said, 'He is my brother.' In the integrity of my heart and the innocence
of my hands I have done this."
Then God said to him in the dream, "Yes, I know that you have done this in the
integrity of your heart, and it was I who kept you from sinning against me;
therefore I did not let you touch her."

Genesis 50:15-17,19,20.

When Joseph's brothers saw that their father was dead, they said, "It may be
that Joseph will hate us and pay us back for all the evil which we did to him."
So they sent a message to Joseph, saying, "Your father gave this command before
he died, 'Say to Joseph, Forgive, I pray you, the transgression of your brothers
and their sin, because they did evil to you.' And now, we pray you, forgive the
transgression of the servants of the God of your father." Joseph wept when
they spoke to him....
Joseph said to them, "Fear not, for am I in the place of God? As for you, you
meant evil against me; but God meant it for good, to bring it about that many
people should be kept alive, as they are today."

The exhibit shows two passages from the Elohist; one selected from the last frame, and the other from Frame # 19 where you were examining the Jahwist's conception of the power of the deity.

Examine especially the second paragraphs in each selection to see if there is a consistency in the Elohist's conception of God's power.

In each group of choices below, two out of the three are incorrect.
Cross out the numbers of the sentences below that make faulty deductions.

A. The importance of the intentions of Abimelech.

1. Abimelech added Sarah to his harem innocently because he believed Abraham; so God was able to forgive Abimelech. In the story God would have been helpless if Abimelech had been a malicious person.

2. In the story Abimelech was really lying about believing that Sarah was Abraham's wife. But God used Abimelech's story as a pretext for forgiving Abimelech.

3. Abimelech's intentions were unimportant. It was God who did not allow Abimelech to sin.

B. The importance of Joseph's brothers' evil against Joseph.

4. Joseph's thought was that his brothers had to ask for forgiveness. The difficulty arises in that forgiveness is a two-way process; if people do not ask for forgiveness, in actuality one does not forgive them.

5. Joseph's thought was: his brothers had intended evil, it is true; but it is God who makes evil things turn out evil or turn out good. In this case God had taken the evil intentions of Joseph's brothers and produced something good.

6. Joseph really hated his brothers, but God in the dream has pointed out that what was apparently evil came from a sincerity of heart; therefore Joseph should not be small and cherish hatred.

C. Conclusions about the consistency in the Elohist's portrayal of the deity's power.

7. The passages are not consistent because with Abimelech, God depends upon his intentions, but with Joseph's brothers God does what he pleases.

8. The passages are consistent in that unless human beings have good intentions God can do nothing.

9. The passages express essentially the same point—that God is absolute Lord over man's intentions and the outcome of these intentions.

ANSWER to Frame # 32

A. The importance of the intentions of Abimelech.

   X. Abimelech added Sarah to his harem innocently because he believed
   Abraham; so God was able to forgive Abimelech. In the story
   God would have been helpless if Abimelech had been a malicious
   person.

   X. In the story Abimelech was really lying about believing that
   Sarah was Abraham's wife. But God used Abimelech's story as a
   pretext for forgiving Abimelech.

   3. Abimelech's intentions were unimportant. It was God who did not
   allow Abimelech to sin.

B. The importance of Joseph's brothers' evil against Joseph.

   X. Joseph's thought was that his brothers had to ask for forgiveness.
   The difficulty arises in that forgiveness is a two-way process; if
   people do not ask for forgiveness, in actuality one does not forgive
   them.

   5. Joseph's thought was: his brothers had intended evil, it is true;
   but it is God who makes evil things turn out evil or turn out good.
   In this case God had taken the evil intentions of Joseph's brothers
   and produced something good.

   X. Joseph really hated his brothers, but God in the dream has pointed
   out that what was apparently evil came from a sincerity of heart;
   therefore Joseph should not be small and cherish hatred.

C. Conclusions about the consistency in the Elohist's portrayal of the
deity's power.

   X. The passages are not consistent because with Abimelech, God depends
   upon his intentions, but with Joseph's brothers God does what he
   pleases.

   X. The passages are consistent in that unless human beings have good
   intentions God can do nothing.

   9. The passages express essentially the same point--that God is
   absolute Lord over man's intentions and the outcome of these
   intentions.

Genesis 22:1-13.

After these things God tested Abraham, and said to him, "Abraham!" And he said, "Here am I." He said, "Take your son, your only son Isaac, whom you love, and go to the land of Moriah, and offer him there as a burnt offering upon one of the mountains of which I shall tell you." So Abraham rose early in the morning, saddled his ass, and took two of his young men with him, and his son Isaac; and he cut the wood for the burnt offering, and arose and went to the place of which God had told him. On the third day Abraham lifted up his eyes and saw the place afar off. Then Abraham said to his young men, "Stay here with the ass; I and the lad will go yonder and worship, and come again to you." And Abraham took the wood of the burnt offering, and laid it on Isaac his son; and he took in his hand the fire and the knife. So they went both of them together. And Isaac said to his father Abraham, "My father!" And he said, "Here I am, my son." He said, "Behold, the fire and the wood; but where is the lamb for a burnt offering?" Abraham said, "God will provide himself the lamb for a burnt offering, my son." So they went both of them together.
When they came to the place of which God had told him, Abraham built an altar there, and laid the wood in order, and bound Isaac his son, and laid him on the altar, upon the wood. Then Abraham put forth his hand, and took the knife to slay his son. But... [God]...called to him from heaven, and said, "Abraham, Abraham!" And he said, "Here am I." He said, "Do not lay your hand on the lad or do anything to him; for now I know that you fear God, seeing you have not withheld your son, your only son, from me." And Abraham lifted up his eyes and looked, and behold, behind him was a ram, caught in a thicket by his horns; and Abraham went and took the ram, and offered it up as a burnt offering instead of his son.

Commentary

This story is one of many which depict Abraham as a devout follower of the deity's commands.
You may remember that Isaac is the only son of Abraham and Sarah.

This part of the story shows especially that the Elohist is a skillful story-teller. We do not have many of the Elohist's stories; it may be that they have been omitted in the final editing of the Pentateuch.

The original reads "But the angel of the LORD called..." I substituted the word God, for in the theory the phrase "angel of the LORD" is regarded as an editorial addition. You can preserve the generalization that in Genesis, the Elohist uses Elohim as the term for the deity.

Frame # 33

Inspect the exhibit on the opposite side to see whether the Elohist continues to emphasize humane standards, as well as the non-human form of the deity.

Place checks before an element that accurately completes a sentence.

1. The test which God proposes to Abraham concerns whether

____ a. Abraham is willing to make a long journey with all the dangers he may encounter.

____ b. Abraham is willing to sacrifice the only son Sarah and he had.

2. Abraham showed his attitude toward God's demands by

____ a. ordering young men to accompany him--a fact showing that Abraham anticipated the dangers and was providing for the defense he might have to make.

____ b. preparing all the necessities for a sacrifice and by taking Isaac along with him.

3. In the kind of story told by the Jahwist by contrast with this story, the deity in speaking to Abraham would probably have

____ a. appeared right there in human form.

____ b. called from heaven.

4. We have been analyzing the stories in the Pentateuch for the points of view of the sources. The ending of this story probably expresses an outlook of the Elohist. If you note how everything is worked out, you would say that by the time of the Elohist

____ a. animal sacrifice replaces human sacrifice.

____ b. animal sacrifice never replaces human sacrifice.

ANSWER to Frame # 33

1. b   2. b   3. a   4. a

The next frame rehearses you on the relative weight given to the ethical in the Elohist's Ten Commandments. If you feel confident about this matter, you may wish to skip to Frame # 35 where you test yourself on your ability to distinguish Elohist material from other sources.

Exodus 34:14,17-23,25,26.= Jahwist	Exodus 20:3,4,7-10,12-17.= Elohist
...you shall worship no other god,...	You shall have no other gods before me.
You shall make for yourself no molten gods.	You shall not make yourself a graven image, or any likeness of anything...
The feast of unleavened bread you shall keep. Seven days you shall eat unleavened bread, as I commanded you, at the time appointed in the month Abib;... All that opens the womb is mine, all your male cattle, the firstlings of cow and sheep. The firstling of an ass you shall redeem with a lamb, or if you will not redeem it you shall break its neck. All the first-born of your sons you shall redeem. And none shall appear before me empty.	
Six days you shall work, but on the seventh day you shall rest; in plowing time and in harvest you shall rest.	You shall not take the name of the LORD your God in vain; for the LORD will not hold him guiltless who takes his name in vain. Remember the sabbath day, to keep it holy. Six days you shall labor, and do all your work; but the seventh day is a sabbath to the LORD your God;...

And you shall observe the feast of weeks, the first fruits of wheat harvest, and the feast of ingathering at the year's end. Three times in the year shall all your males appear before the LORD God, the God of Israel....
   You shall not offer the blood of my
   sacrifice with leaven;
neither shall the sacrifice of the feast of the passover be left until the morning.
   The first of the first fruits of
   your ground you shall bring to the
   house of the LORD your God.
You shall not boil a kid in its mother's milk.
	Honor your father and your mother,...
	   You shall not kill.
	You shall not commit adultery.
	   You shall not steal.
	You shall not bear false witness against your neighbor.
	   You shall not covet...anything that
	   is your neighbor's.

The exhibit repeats one used for Frame # 25. Examine the material again to note the relative emphases placed upon the ceremonial and the ethical in the right-hand column.

Since you have already classified [in Frame # 25] which of the Elohist's Ten Commandments are ethical, the exercise below now asks you to select from the phrases the <u>reasoning</u> behind each commandment.

Place a check before the element that completes each statement correctly.

1. No gods are to be preferred over Jahweh nor are images of God to be made--a ceremonial rule because

    ___ a. it injures other people when you break these rules.

    ___ b. **neither practice is appropriate to the worship of Jahweh.**

2. Using the name of Jahweh in vain and working on the Sabbath have to do with ceremonial matters because

    ___ a. these practices are not regarded as suitable for Jahweh worshippers.

    ___ b. the sound of the word Jahweh and the viewing of work on the Sabbath might injure the ears or eyes of other Hebrews.

3. The dishonoring of one's parents and having intercourse with another's mate are ethical rules because

    ___ a. they injure the integrity of the family as an institution.

    ___ b. **such behavior is not nice.**

4. Killing and stealing break ethical rules in that

    ___ a. the acts take something valuable from another human being--his life or his property.

    ___ b. people feel strange if they do these things.

5. Bearing false witness offends against ethical rules in that

    ___ a. people simply don't do that sort of thing in good society.

    ___ b. it makes impossible the trust in one another that creates common bonds.

6. The rule against coveting [a command about one's attitude rather than act] has to do with ethics because

    ___ a. it would be a strange response for one person to desire what belongs to another.

    ___ b. desire might lead one to injure another in order to secure the desired item.

1. No gods are to be preferred over Jahweh nor are images of God to be made--a ceremonial rule because

    ___ a. it injures other people when you break these rules.

    ✓ b. neither practice is appropriate to the worship of Jahweh.

2. Using the name of Jahweh in vain and working on the Sabbath have to do with ceremonial matters because

    ✓ a. these practices are not regarded as suitable for Jahweh worshippers.

    ___ b. the sound of the word Jahweh and the viewing of work on the Sabbath might injure the ears or eyes of other Hebrews.

3. The dishonoring of one's parents and having intercourse with another's mate are ethical rules because

    ✓ a. they injure the integrity of the family as an institution.

    ___ b. such behavior is not nice.

4. Killing and stealing break ethical rules in that

    ✓ a. the acts take something valuable from another human being--his life or his property.

    ___ b. people feel strange if they do these things.

5. Bearing false witness offends against ethical rules in that

    ___ a. people simply don't do that sort of thing in good society.

    ✓ b. it makes impossible the trust in one another that creates common bonds.

6. The rule against coveting [a command about one's attitude rather than act] has to do with ethics because

    ___ a. it would be a strange response for one person to desire what belongs to another.

    ✓ b. desire might lead one to injure another in order to secure the desired item.

A. Genesis 26:6-13.

So Isaac dwelt in Gerar. When the men of the place asked him about his wife, he said, "She is my sister"; for he feared to say, "My wife," thinking, "lest the men of the place should kill me for the sake of Rebekah"; because she was fair to look upon. When he had been there a long time, Abimelech king of the Philistines looked out of a window and saw Isaac fondling Rebekah his wife. So Abimelech called Isaac, and said, "Behold, she is your wife; how then could you say, 'She is my sister'?" Isaac said to him, "Because I thought, 'Lest I die because of her.'" Abimelech said, "What is this you have done to us? One of the people might easily have lain with your wife, and you would have brought guilt upon us." So Abimelech warned all the people, saying, "Whoever touches this man or his wife shall be put to death." And Isaac sowed in that land, and reaped in the same year a hundredfold. The LORD blessed him, and the man became rich, and gained more and more until he became very wealthy.

B. Exodus 8:5,8,12-15. [A selection from the story of the 10 plagues upon the Egyptians to force Pharaoh to allow the Israelites to leave.]
And the LORD said to Moses, "Say to Aaron, 'Stretch out your hand with your rod over the rivers, over the canals, and over the pools, and cause frogs to come upon the land of Egypt!'" ...Then Pharaoh called Moses and Aaron, and said, "Entreat the LORD to take away the frogs from me and from my people; and I will let the people go to sacrifice to the LORD."
...So Moses and Aaron went out from Pharaoh; and Moses cried to the LORD concerning the frogs, as he had agreed with Pharaoh. And the LORD did according to the word of Moses; the frogs died out of the houses and court- yards and out of the fields. And they gathered them together in heaps, and the land stank. But when Pharaoh saw that there was a respite, <u>he hardened his heart</u>, and would not listen to them; as the LORD had said.

C. Exodus 10:27; 11:1-3. [Another selection from the story of the 10 plagues.]

But <u>the LORD hardened Pharaoh's heart</u>, and he would not let them go.

The LORD said to Moses, "Yet one plague more I will bring upon Pharaoh and upon Egypt; afterwards he will let you go hence; when he lets you go, he will drive you away completely. Speak now in the hearing of the people, that they ask, every man of his neighbor and every woman of her neighbor, jewelry of silver and of gold." And the LORD gave the people favor in the sight of the Egyptians. Moreover, the man Moses was very great in the land of Egypt, in the sight of Pharaoh's servants and in the sight of the people.

The Jahwist, Elohist, and Priestly sources are represented in the exhibit by one passage each.
Test yourself by answering the questions below; it is best first to find the Jahwist and the Elohist, for the remaining passage belongs to the Priestly source.

1. Reasons for assigning passage "A:"

    a. Jahweh is the term for the deity. Does this fact exclude the Elohist or the Priestly sources? ___

    Why? _____

    b. Isaac, one of the early heroes of Israel, told the king of the Philistines that Rebekah was his sister and she was not. Does the fact that the passage does not hide a human weakness help to classify the passage? ___

    Why? _____

    _____

2. Reasons for assigning passage "B:"

    a. Jahweh is the term for the deity. Does this fact exclude the Elohist or the Priestly sources? ___

    Why? _____

    b. Pharaoh hardens his own heart [becomes obstinate]. In other words, the deity does not make Pharaoh's choice for him. Does this help to classify the passage? ___

    Why? _____

    _____

3. Reasons for assigning passage "C:"

    a. Jahweh is the term for the deity. Does this fact exclude the Elohist or the Priestly sources? ___

    Why? _____

    b. Jahweh hardens Pharaoh's heart [makes him obstinate]. In other words, the deity makes the choice for Pharaoh. Does this help to classify the passage? ___

    Why? _____

    _____

4. Passage "A" = (Jahwist)(Elohist)(Priestly); Passage "B" = (Jahwist)(Elohist)(Priestly); Passage "C" = (Jahwist)(Elohist)(Priestly).

1. Reasons for assigning passage "A:"

   a. Jahweh is the term for the deity. Does this fact exclude the Elohist or the Priestly sources? *Yes*

   Why? *The Elohist and the Priestly sources do not generally use Jahweh in Genesis.*

   b. Isaac, one of the early heroes of Israel, told the king of the Philistines that Rebekah was his sister and she was not. Does the fact that the passage does not hide a human weakness help to classify the passage? *Yes*

   Why? *A student wrote as follows: Isaac as a hero is shown to have human weakness, for he was afraid to say that Rebekah was his wife. The Jahwist does not worry that in his stories the early heroes display such weaknesses.*

2. Reasons for assigning passage "B:"

   a. Jahweh is the term for the deity. Does this fact exclude the Elohist or the Priestly sources? *No*

   Why? *Both the Elohist and the Priestly sources can use Jahweh in Exodus.*

   b. Pharaoh hardens his own heart [becomes obstinate]. In other words, the deity does not make Pharaoh's choice for him. Does this help to classify the passage? *Yes*

   Why? *In the Elohist the deity is more apt to make man's choices for him.*

3. Reasons for assigning passage "C:"

   a. Jahweh is the term for the deity. Does this fact exclude the Elohist or the Priestly sources? *No*

   Why? *Both the Elohist and the Priestly sources can use Jahweh in Exodus.*

   b. Jahweh hardens Pharaoh's heart [makes him obstinate]. In other words, the deity makes the choice for Pharaoh. Does this help to classify the passage? *Yes*

   Why? *A student wrote as follows: In the story Jahweh hardened Pharaoh's heart which shows that he is all-powerful and has command over man's intentions. This is the Elohist's emphasis on the power of the deity.*

4. Passage "A" = (<u>Jahwist</u>)(Elohist)(Priestly); Passage "B" = (Jahwist)(Elohist) (<u>Priestly</u>); Passage "C" = (Jahwist)(<u>Elohist</u>)(Priestly).

Exodus 20:3,4,7-10,12-17.= Elohist	Deuteronomy 5:7,8,11-14,16-21.
You shall have no other gods before me.	You shall have no other gods before me.
You shall not make yourself a graven image, or any likeness of anything...	You shall not make for yourself a graven image, or any likeness of anything...
You shall not take the name of the LORD your God in vain; for the LORD will not hold him guiltless who takes his name in vain.	You shall not take the name of the LORD your God in vain: for the LORD will not hold him guiltless who takes his name in vain.
Remember the sabbath day, to keep it holy. Six days you shall labor, and do all your work; but the seventh day is a sabbath to the LORD your God;...	Observe the sabbath day, to keep it holy, as the LORD your God commanded you. Six days you shall labor, and do all your work; but the seventh day is a sabbath to the LORD your God;...
Honor your father and your mother,...	Honor your father and your mother,...
You shall not kill.	You shall not kill.
You shall not commit adultery.	Neither shall you commit adultery.
You shall not steal.	Neither shall you steal.
You shall not bear false witness against your neighbor.	Neither shall you bear false witness against your neighbor.
You shall not covet...anything that is your neighbor's.	Neither shall you covet...anything that is your neighbor's.

The theory called *Source Analysis of the Pentateuch* considers the book of Deuteronomy [not necessarily all of the book] as the product of *another* school of thought. This source is known as the Deuteronomist.
Inspect the two sets of commandments in the exhibit for major differences in thought.

Place a check before elements that correctly complete a sentence.

1. In the wording of the Ten Commandments the Elohist and the Deuteronomist

   ____ a. differ somewhat in style but not in substance.

   ____ b. differ somewhat in substance but not in style.

2. In the use of terms for the deity

   ____ a. both the Elohist and the Deuteronomist use the term Jahweh.

   ____ b. the Elohist uses the generic term but the Deuteronomist employs the specific term.

3. Therefore with respect to discriminating between the Elohist and the Deuteronomist

   ____ a. one could use the different term for the deity but not the substance of the commandments as identification.

   ____ b. one could use neither the term for the deity nor the substance of the commandments as identification.

ANSWER to Frame # 36

1. a	2. a	3. b

There are differences between the Deuteronomist and the Elohist, as well as the Jahwist, that can be identified.

Exodus 20:22-24.   A passage from the Elohist

And the LORD said to Moses, "Thus you shall say to the people of Israel: 'You have seen for yourselves that I have talked with you from heaven. You shall not make gods of silver to be with me, nor shall you make for yourselves gods of gold. An altar of earth you shall make for me and sacrifice on it your burnt offerings and your peace offerings, your sheep and your oxen; in every place where I cause my name to be remembered I will come to you and bless you.'"

Deuteronomy 12:8-18.

You shall not do according to all that we are doing here this day, every man doing whatever is right in his own eyes; for you have not as yet come to the rest and to the inheritance which the LORD your God gives you.

[Rules for the new situation]

But when you go over the Jordan, and live in the land which the LORD your God gives you to inherit, and when he gives you rest from all your enemies round about, so that you live in safety, then to the place which the LORD your God will choose, to make his name dwell there, thither you shall bring all that I command you: your burnt offerings and your sacrifices, your tithes and the offering that you present, and all your votive offerings which you vow to the LORD. And you shall rejoice before the LORD your God....Take heed that you do not offer your burnt offerings at every place that you see; but at the place which the LORD will choose in one of your tribes, there you shall offer your burnt offerings, and there you shall do all that I am commanding you.

[Provision for food that is not sacred]

However, you may slaughter and eat flesh within any of your towns, as much as you desire,...the unclean and the clean may eat of it, as of the gazelle and as of the hart. Only you shall not eat the blood; you shall pour it out upon the earth like water. You may not eat within your towns the tithe of your grain or of your wine or of your oil, or the firstlings of your herd or of your flock, or any of your votive offerings which you vow, or your freewill offerings, or the offering that you present; but you shall eat them before the LORD your God in the place which the LORD your God will choose,...and you shall rejoice before the LORD your God in all that you undertake.

Compare the passages from the Elohist and the Deuteronomist in the exhibit to identify ideas about sacrifice.

Underline the elements below that complete correctly the statements about the passages in the exhibit.

1. The Elohist implies that sacrifice can be made at (many places) (one place only).

2. The Deuteronomist holds that things which were right at one time (are still right)(must be changed).

3. The Deuteronomist says that sacrifice can be made at (many places) (one place only).

4. Any meat that is offered to God in a sacrifice is eaten afterward. If the Deuteronomist's rule about places of sacrifice were followed, *and the previous law held that if one eats meat, one must sacrifice,* (one would have to have one's own priest)(meat would disappear from the diet of many since distances would limit trips to the one place).

5. So the Deuteronomist is concerned about supplementing the traditional rules about sacred and non-sacred foods. The provision he makes is that (one must sacrifice all meat since there are many acceptable altars)(one must not sacrifice if one cannot bring the animal to the one place, but killing for food is permissible and the food is not treated as though it were sacred).

6. A potential source of food is forbidden. (Blood must not be eaten) (Non-sacred food must not be eaten at all).

7. If the Deuteronomist's rule about places suitable for sacrifice were followed it would have a significant effect upon the priesthood of the time. (Many priests would be employed at many shrines throughout the land)(The priests and their teachings could be brought under centralized control).

1. The Elohist implies that sacrifice can be made at (<u>many places</u>) (one place only).

2. The Deuteronomist holds that things which were right at one time (are still right)(<u>must be changed</u>).

3. The Deuteronomist says that sacrifice can be made at (many places) (<u>one place only</u>).

4. Any meat that is offered to God in a sacrifice is eaten afterward. If the Deuteronomist's rule about places of sacrifice were followed, *and the previous law held that if one eats meat, one must sacrifice,* (one would have to have one's own priest)(<u>meat would disappear from the diet of many since distances would limit trips to the one place</u>).

5. So the Deuteronomist is concerned about supplementing the traditional rules about sacred and non-sacred foods. The provision he makes is that (one must sacrifice all meat since there are many acceptable altars)(<u>one must not sacrifice if one cannot bring the animal to the one place, but killing for food is permissible and the food is not treated as though it were sacred</u>).

6. A potential source of food is forbidden. (<u>Blood must not be eaten</u>) (Non-sacred food must not be eaten at all).

7. If the Deuteronomist's rule about places suitable for sacrifice were followed it would have a significant effect upon the priesthood of the time. (Many priests would be employed at many shrines throughout the land)(<u>The priests and their teachings could be brought under centralized control</u>).

II Kings 23:4,5,7-9,13,15,24.

And the king commanded Hilkiah, the high priest, and the priests of the second order, and the keepers of the threshold, to bring out of the temple of the LORD all the vessels made for Baal, for Asherah, and for all the host of heaven;... And he deposed the idolatrous priests whom the kings of Judah had ordained to burn incense in the high places at the cities of Judah and round about Jerusalem; ...And he broke down the houses of the cult prostitutes which were in the house of the LORD, where the women wove hangings for the Asherah. And he brought all the priests out of the cities of Judah, and defiled the high places where the priests had burned incense,...However, the priests of the high places did not come up to the altar of the LORD in Jerusalem, but they ate unleavened bread among their brethren....And the king defiled the high places that were east of Jerusalem, to the south of the mount of corruption, which Solomon the king of Israel had built for Ashtoreth the abomination of the Sidonians, and for Chemosh the abomination of Moab, and for Milcom the abomination of the Ammonites.... Moreover the altar at Bethel, the high place erected by Jeroboam the son of Nebat, who made Israel to sin, that altar with the high place he pulled down and he broke in pieces its stones, crushing them to dust; also he burned the Asherah....
Moreover Josiah put away the mediums and the wizards and the teraphim and the idols and all the abominations that were seen in the land of Judah and in Jerusalem, that he might establish the words of the law which were written in the book that Hilkiah the priest found in the house of the LORD.

Deuteronomy 12:2,3; 16:21,22; 18:10,11.

You shall surely destroy all the places where the nations whom you shall dis-possess served their gods, upon the high mountains and upon the hills and under every green tree; you shall tear down their altars, and dash in pieces their pillars, and burn their Asherim with fire; you shall hew down the graven images of their gods, and destroy their name out of that place....
You shall not plant any tree as an Asherah beside the altar of the LORD your God which you shall make. And you shall not set up a pillar, which the LORD your God hates....
There shall not be found among you any one who burns his son or his daughter as an offering, any one who practices divination, a soothsayer, or an augur, or a sorcerer, or a charmer, or a medium, or a wizard, or a necromancer.

A reform in ceremonial practices is demanded in Deuteronomy. In the exhibit on the opposite page passages from Second Kings are quoted. By answering the questions below, compare the demands in Deuteronomy with the reforms carried out by King Josiah.

Following are statements of reforms described in II Kings. Circle the number of any statement of a reform that corresponds to the demands in Deuteronomy.

1. Ceremonial objects dedicated to Gods other than Jahweh [other Gods such as a Baal, Asherah, or the host of heaven] are brought out of the Temple.

2. High places were defiled.

3. People destroy the houses of sacred prostitutes who were associated with the Temple of Jahweh [certain practices of a fertility religion had been imported from other religious traditions].

4. Images such as the teraphim are destroyed.

Place a check below before the statement that seems a more probable conclusion from the comparison of Deuteronomy with II Kings.

5. In the time of King Josiah the scene is set for the return to the worship of the one God, Jahweh;

____ a. but the way the reform is carried out seems quite unlike the measures urged in the book of Deuteronomy.

____ b. the reforms seem generally to be the ones asked for in Deuteronomy.

ANSWER to Frame # 38

1, 2, and 4 correspond to the demands in Deuteronomy.

5. b is more probable.

II Kings 22:3-6. [*King Josiah in 621 B.C. orders the repair of Jahweh's Temple.*]

In the eighteenth year of King Josiah, the king sent Shaphan the son of Azaliah, son of Meshullam, the secretary, to the house of the LORD, saying, "Go up to Hilkiah the high priest, that he may reckon the amount of the money which has been brought into the house of the LORD, which the keepers of the threshold have collected from the people; and let it be given... to the workmen who are at the house of the LORD, repairing the house, that is, to the carpenters, and to the builders, and to the masons, as well as for buying timber and quarried stone to repair the house."

II Kings 22:8,10. [*A book is found in the temple.*]

And Hilkiah the high priest said to Shaphan the secretary, "I have found the book of the law in the house of the LORD." And Hilkiah gave the book to Shaphan, and he read it....Then Shaphan the secretary told the king, "Hilkiah the priest has given me a book." And Shaphan read it before the king.

II Kings 22:11-13. [*The reaction of King Josiah.*]

And when the king heard the words of the book of the law, he rent his clothes. And the king commanded Hilkiah the priest, and Ahikam the son of Shapan, and Achbor the son of Micaiah, and Shaphan the secretary, and Asaiah the king's servant, saying, "Go, inquire of the LORD for me, and for the people, and for all Judah, concerning the words of this book that has been found; for great is the wrath of the LORD that is kindled against us, because our fathers have not obeyed the words of this book, to do according to all that is written concerning us."

[*In II Kings 22:14-20 it is recorded that Huldah the prophetess authenticated the book as Jahweh's words.*]

II Kings 23:1-3. [*The book is read before the people.*]

Then the king sent, and all the elders of Judah and Jerusalem were gathered to him. And the king went up to the house of the LORD, and with him all the men of Judah and all the inhabitants of Jerusalem, and the priests and the prophets, all the people, both small and great; and he read in their hearing all the words of the book of the covenant which had been found in the house of the LORD. And the king stood by the pillar and made a covenant before the LORD, to walk after the LORD and to keep his commandments and his testimonies and his statutes, with all his heart and all his soul, to perform the words of this covenant that were written in this book; and all the people joined in the covenant.

Observe the details of the discovery of a book found in the Temple of Jahweh during King Josiah's reign, details found in the passages quoted in the exhibit.

Eliminate the false descriptions of the events in the exhibit by crossing out appropriate numbers of sentences below.

1. King Josiah ordered a repair of the Temple [called the "house" of Jahweh].

2. The high priest sent news to King Josiah that a book bearing the title "Deuteronomy" had been discovered in the Temple.

3. Since King Josiah knew that Deuteronomy was in the Old Testament he immediately asked that the book found in the Temple be treated with great respect.

4. King Josiah was so struck by the content of the book of the law as it was read to him that he tore his clothes out of grief that his people had forsaken the law.

5. The king asked that the book's authenticity be investigated.

6. Josiah pledged to follow "with all his heart and soul" the demands of the book found in the Temple.

ANSWER to Frame # 39

2 and 3 are false.

You have seen now the evidence which leads scholars to believe that the book of Deuteronomy corresponds generally to the book found in the Temple during the repair ordered by King Josiah.

Following frames analyze characteristics of selected passages from Deuteronomy.

Exodus	Deuteronomy 24:10-18.
	When you make your neighbor a loan of any sort, you shall not go into his house to fetch his pledge. You shall stand outside, and the man to whom you make the loan shall bring the pledge out to you. And if he is a poor man, you shall not sleep in his pledge; when the sun goes down, you shall restore to him the pledge that he may sleep in his cloak and bless you; and it shall be righteousness to you before the LORD your God.
22:26,27. If ever you take your neighbor's garment in pledge, you shall restore it to him before the sun goes down: for that is his only covering, it is his mantle for his body; in what else shall he sleep? And if he cries to me, I will hear, for I am compassionate.	
	You shall not oppress a hired servant who is poor and needy, whether he is one of your brethren or one of the sojourners who are in your land within your towns; you shall give him his hire on the day he earns it, before the sun goes down (for he is poor, and sets his heart upon it); lest he cry against you to the LORD, and it be sin in you.
	The fathers shall not be put to death for the children, nor shall the children be put to death for the fathers; every man shall be put to death for his own sin.
23:6,7,9. You shall not pervert the justice due to your poor in his suit. Keep far from a false charge, and do not slay the innocent and righteous, for I will not acquit the wicked.... You shall not oppress a stranger; you know the heart of a stranger, for you were strangers in the land of Egypt.	You shall not pervert the justice due to the sojourner or to the fatherless, or take a widow's garment in pledge; but you shall remember that you were a slave in Egypt and the LORD your God redeemed you from there; therefore I command you to do this.

In Deuteronomy few "stories" are to be found for analysis. But an inspection of laws may yield perspectives of the writers of Deuteronomy.

The left-hand column in the exhibit contains laws often assigned to the Elohist. Compare the material in Deuteronomy with that from Exodus in order to discover refinements of conscience in Deuteronomy.

On the left-hand side below you will find statements about the laws in Exodus. You are to make a correct comparison with the material from Deuteronomy by drawing a line to the appropriate sentence in the right-hand column.

Example:

1. The requirement in Exodus states that you cannot keep overnight a garment pledged as security for a loan.

a. Deuteronomy agrees with this and there is no further refinement.
b. Deuteronomy adds that you may not shame a person by going into his home to take the pledge. Thus the borrower's dignity is considered.

2. In Exodus nothing is said about when the wages of a laborer must be paid.

a. Deuteronomy thus is showing a refinement by refusing to allow the employer to retain [and possibly profit by] the wages that properly belong to the laborer.
b. Deuteronomy thus is protecting the employer who does not have to pay out wages until the laborer demands them.

3. In Exodus nothing is said about punishment's being restricted to the guilty *individual*.

a. Deuteronomy is asking that just punishment be meted out only to the guilty individual; no more can the family be allowed to suffer because of the guilt of one member of the family.
b. Deuteronomy shows the same feeling. The innocent members of a family should suffer together with the guilty member of the family because the family has failed to correct the tendencies of its irresponsible member.

4. In Exodus a reason for treating well the poor, the innocent, the righteous and the stranger, is that Israel was once a stranger in Egypt.

a. In Deuteronomy no mention is made of Israel's history in Egypt because it is a poor principle to wound the pride of anyone by asking them to recall their humble origins.
b. Perhaps "slave" is stronger than "stranger" in asking for a humility that will lead to more compassion for others.

1. The requirement in Exodus states that you cannot keep overnight a garment pledged as security for a loan.

a. Deuteronomy agrees with this and there is no further refinement.
Ⓑ. Deuteronomy adds that you may not shame a person by going into his home to take the pledge. Thus the borrower's dignity is considered.

---

2. In Exodus nothing is said about when the wages of a laborer must be paid.

Ⓐ. Deuteronomy thus is showing a refinement by refusing to allow the employer to retain [and possibly profit by] the wages that properly belong to the laborer.
b. Deuteronomy thus is protecting the employer who does not have to pay out wages until the laborer demands them.

---

3. In Exodus nothing is said about punishment's being restricted to the guilty *individual*.

Ⓐ. Deuteronomy is asking that just punishment be meted out only to the guilty individual; no more can the family be allowed to suffer because of the guilt of one member of the family.
b. Deuteronomy shows the same feeling. The innocent members of a family should suffer together with the guilty member of the family because the family has failed to correct the tendencies of its irresponsible member.

---

4. In Exodus a reason for treating well the poor, the innocent, the righteous and the stranger, is that Israel was once a stranger in Egypt.

a. In Deuteronomy no mention is made of Israel's history in Egypt because it is a poor principle to wound the pride of anyone by asking them to recall their humble origins.
Ⓑ. Perhaps "slave" is stronger than "stranger" in asking for a humility that will lead to more compassion for others.

Frame # 41

Some have been taught that the Old Testament presents a God one should fear, while the New Testament tells about a God one should love. Inspect the passages below to see whether such a generalization fits the teachings of Deuteronomy.

A. Deuteronomy 6:4,5. Hear, O Israel: The LORD our God is one LORD; and you shall love the LORD your God with all your heart, and with all your soul, and with all your might.

B. Deuteronomy 6:24. And the LORD commanded us to do all these statutes, to fear the LORD our God, for our good always, that he might preserve us alive, as at this day.

C. Deuteronomy 8:19,20. And if you forget the LORD your God and go after other gods and serve them and worship them, I solemnly warn you this day that you shall surely perish. Like the nations that the LORD makes to perish before you, so shall you perish, because you would not obey the voice of the LORD your God.

D. Deuteronomy 26:16. This day the LORD your God commands you to do these statutes and ordinances; you shall therefore be careful to do them with all your heart and with all your soul.

Place checks below before the clauses that correctly complete each statement below.

1. Deuteronomy suggests several reasons why men should obey God. The passages above note specifically that

____ a. men by obedience will get to heaven;

____ b. men should love God;

____ c. men are commanded to fear God;

____ d. if men do not obey they will perish;

____ e. and disobedience will lead to the death of the nation.

2. Deuteronomy also states the level of intensity that should govern obedience. Men should respond to God

____ a. coolly.

____ b. with all their heart and all their soul.

1. Deuteronomy suggests several reasons why men should obey God.
   The passages above note specifically that

   ___ a. men by obedience will get to heaven;

   ✓ b. men should love God;

   ✓ c. men are commanded to fear God;

   ✓ d. if men do not obey they will perish;

   ✓ e. and disobedience will lead to the death of the nation.

2. Deuteronomy also states the level of intensity that should govern
   obedience. Men should respond to God

   ___ a. coolly.

   ✓ b. with all their heart and all their soul.

Deuteronomy is remarkable also in that the book provides some discussion of the problem of unjust suffering.

Examine the passages below to see in what manner the thinking of Deuteronomy supplies the pre-conditions of the discovery of the problem of unjust suffering.

A. Deuteronomy 21:15-17. If a man has two wives, the one loved and the other disliked, and they have borne him children, both the loved and the disliked, and if the first-born son is hers that is disliked, then on the day when he assigns his possessions as an inheritance to his sons, he may not treat the son of the loved as the first-born in preference to the son of the disliked, who is the first-born, but he shall acknowledge the first-born, the son of the disliked, by giving him a double portion of all that he has....the right of the first-born is his.

B. Deuteronomy 24:14,15. You shall not oppress a hired servant who is poor and needy, whether he is one of your brethren or one of the sojourners who are in your land within your towns; you shall give him his hire on the day he earns it, before the sun goes down (for he is poor, and sets his heart upon it); lest he cry against you to the LORD, and it be sin in you.

C. Deuteronomy 24:16. The fathers shall not be put to death for the children, nor shall the children be put to death for the fathers; every man shall be put to death for his own sin.

Place a check before the reasoning that correctly shows how a specific pre-condition is fulfilled in Deuteronomy.

1. It must be supposed that justice exists in life.

____ a. Passage B implies that Jahweh interests himself in justice even to powerless classes. This suggests a faith in ultimate justice in life.

____ b. Passage C discusses who is to be put to death. Since capital punishment is accepted in ancient life, this passage implies that justice in life can be depended upon.

2. It must be thought that whether justice is done *to the individual* is the crucial test of justice in life.

____ a. Passage C insists that members of a family cannot be lumped together when an individual is guilty. Thus justice to the individual is regarded as crucial.

____ b. Passage A is concerned that a wife should be disliked even though she is the first wife. It suggests a family conference in order that the husband and wife learn to communicate.

3. There must be sensitivity to the actual conditions of individual lives.

____ a. Passage A forbids disinheriting the first-born son. Sensitivity to rejection of the first wife, probably older and less loved, is implied; for one injures a wife by mistreating the son.

____ b. Passage A is concerned about the feelings of members of a family when only one is guilty.

1. It must be supposed that justice exists in life.

   ✓ a. Passage B implies that Jahweh interests himself in justice even to powerless classes. This suggests a faith in ultimate justice in life.

   ___ b. Passage C discusses who is to be put to death. Since capital punishment is accepted in ancient life, this passage implies that justice in life can be depended upon.

2. It must be thought that whether justice is done *to the individual* is the crucial test of justice in life.

   ✓ a. Passage C insists that members of a family cannot be lumped together when an individual is guilty. Thus justice to the individual is regarded as crucial.

   ___ b. Passage A is concerned that a wife should be disliked even though she is the first wife. It suggests a family conference in order that the husband and wife learn to communicate.

3. There must be sensitivity to the actual conditions of individual lives.

   ✓ a. Passage A forbids disinheriting the first-born son. Sensitivity to rejection of the first wife, probably older and less loved, is implied; for one injures a wife by mistreating the son.

   ___ b. Passage A is concerned about the feelings of members of a family when only one is guilty.

The tradition of Israel narrates great difficulties in that period after Israel's escape from Egypt. Inspect the passages below to see how Deuteronomy uses that period several centuries previous, to justify God's allowing Israel to suffer.

Deuteronomy 8:

2. And you shall remember all the way which the LORD your God has led you these forty years in the wilderness, that he might humble you, testing you to know what was in your heart, whether you would keep his commandments or not.
3. And he humbled you and let you hunger and fed you with manna, which you did not know, nor did your fathers know; that he might make you know that man does not live by bread alone, but that man lives by everything that proceeds out of the mouth of the LORD.
4. Your clothing did not wear out upon you, and your foot did not swell, these forty years. 5. Know then in your heart that, as a man disciplines his son, the LORD your God disciplines you.

Circle the numbers of sentences below that analyze correctly Deuteronomy's viewpoint about unjust suffering.

The example of suffering selected:

1. Verses 2-5 use problems of endurance even in the midst of hunger.

2. Verses 2-5 use the problems of war and such illnesses as leprosy.

Comments on the problem of unjust suffering:

3. Suffering can be used as a test of obedience.

4. In verse 3, the point is that Israel did not know about manna [a kind of food]; thus *ignorance* often leads to suffering.

5. Some pain occurs as the price of learning; thus suffering may be a kind of discipline, according to verse 5.

6. Some suffering shows what counts most; thus Israel learned that dependence upon Jahweh was even more important than bread.

7. Verse 3 points out that life is not worthwhile if man does not have bread; values in life are made possible *only* when bodily needs are taken care of.

ANSWER to Frame # 43

1, 3, 5, and 6 are correct.

A. Deuteronomy 26:4-10. Then the priest shall take the basket [containing the fruits harvested] from your hand, and set it down before the altar of the LORD your God.

And you shall make response before the LORD your God, "A wandering Aramean was my father; and he went down into Egypt and sojourned there, few in number; and there he became a nation, great, mighty, and populous. And the Egyptians treated us harshly, and afflicted us, and laid upon us hard bondage. Then we cried to the LORD the God of our fathers, and the LORD heard our voice, and saw our affliction, our toil, and our oppression; and the LORD brought us out of Egypt with a mighty hand and an outstretched arm, with great terror, with signs and wonders; and he brought us into this place and gave us this land, a land flowing with milk and honey. And behold, now I bring the first of the fruit of the ground, which thou, O LORD, hast given me." And you shall set it down before the LORD your God, and worship before the LORD your God.

B. Deuteronomy 7:6-8. For you are a people holy to the LORD your God; the LORD your God has chosen you to be a people for his own possession, out of all the peoples that are on the face of the earth. It was not because you were more in number than any other people that the LORD set his love upon you and chose you, for you were the fewest of all peoples; but it is because the LORD loves you, and is keeping the oath which he swore to your fathers, that the LORD has brought you out with a mighty hand, and redeemed you from the house of bondage, from the hand of Pharaoh king of Egypt.

C. Deuteronomy 9:4-6. Do not say in your heart, after the LORD your God has thrust them [other nations] out before you, "It is because of my righteousness that the LORD has brought me in to possess this land"; whereas it is because of the wickedness of these nations that the LORD is driving them out before you. Not because of your righteousness or the uprightness of your heart are you going in to possess their land; but because of the wickedness of these nations the LORD your God is driving them out from before you, and that he may confirm the word which the LORD swore to your fathers, to Abraham, to Isaac, and to Jacob.

Know therefore, that the LORD your God is not giving you this good land to possess because of your righteousness; for you are a stubborn people.

Deuteronomy emphasizes that Jahweh, and Jahweh alone, is Israel's God. In 6:5 a statement appears that is sometimes called the "creed" of Judaism: "Hear, O Israel: The LORD our God is one LORD;..."
Passage "A" in the exhibit gives a liturgy stating the special relationship between Israel and Jahweh.
Inspect passages "B" and "C" as well for the reasons behind Jahweh's choice of Israel.

Circle the letter of the sentence that completes correctly the thought about Jahweh's relationship to Israel.

1. In Passage "A" Deuteronomy states a relationship between Jahweh and the land in which Israel [in Deuteronomy's time] resides.

    a. Jahweh delivered Israel from bondage in Egypt and gave them the land "flowing with milk and honey."

    b. After Jahweh had seen that Israel had fought for and won a land "flowing with milk and honey" he graciously agreed to become their God.

2. Passage "B" states the relationship between the numbers [importance] of the people of Israel and Jahweh's choice of them.

    a. When Jahweh saw how numerous the people were, he joined them because of Israel's obvious importance.

    b. Jahweh promised Israel protection out of his relationship to their ancestors, and he loves Israel, even though they are not numerous.

3. Passage "C" gives the ideas of Deuteronomy about the uprightness of Israel as a factor in Jahweh's choice.

    a. Israel was a righteous people, and God responded to them because of this uprightness.

    b. Far from being righteous, Israel is known to Jahweh as a stubborn people.

4. Others had taught before Deuteronomy was produced that Israel was a chosen nation. The distinctive thing that Deuteronomy is teaching is that

    a. Israel is the chosen nation of Jahweh because of the unusual devotion Israel has shown Jahweh; when they were in bondage, they cried for deliverance not to the Egyptian god but to Jahweh, and in gratitude he delivered Israel.

    b. Israel's position as the chosen people of Jahweh did not rest on any merit that Israel possessed but on the initiative of Jahweh; Jahweh chose them out of his own nature and purposes.

ANSWER to Frame # 44

1. In Passage "A" Deuteronomy states a relationship between Jahweh and the land in which Israel [in Deuteronomy's time] resides.

(ⓐ). Jahweh delivered Israel from bondage in Egypt and gave them the land "flowing with milk and honey."

b. After Jahweh had seen that Israel had fought for and won a land "flowing with milk and honey" he graciously agreed to become their God.

2. Passage "B" states the relationship between the numbers [importance] of the people of Israel and Jahweh's choice of them.

a. When Jahweh saw how numerous the people were, he joined them because of Israel's obvious importance.

(ⓑ). Jahweh promised Israel protection out of his relationship to their ancestors, and he loves Israel, even though they are not numerous.

3. Passage "C" gives the ideas of Deuteronomy about the uprightness of Israel as a factor in Jahweh's choice.

a. Israel was a righteous people, and God responded to them because of this uprightness.

(ⓑ). Far from being righteous, Israel is known to Jahweh as a stubborn people.

4. Others had taught before Deuteronomy was produced that Israel was a chosen nation. The distinctive thing that Deuteronomy is teaching is that

a. Israel is the chosen nation of Jahweh because of the unusual devotion Israel has shown Jahweh; when they were in bondage, they cried for deliverance not to the Egyptian god but to Jahweh, and in gratitude he delivered Israel.

(ⓑ). Israel's position as the chosen people of Jahweh did not rest on any merit that Israel possessed but on the initiative of Jahweh; Jahweh chose them out of his own nature and purposes.

A.

And now, Israel, what does the LORD your God require of you, but to fear the LORD your God, to walk in all his ways, to love him, to serve the LORD your God with all your heart and with all your soul,...

B.

Then Moses said to God, "If I come to the people of Israel and say to them, 'The God of your fathers has sent me to you,' and they ask me, 'What is his name?' what shall I say to them?" God said to Moses, "I AM WHO I AM." And he said, "Say this to the people of Israel, 'I AM has sent me to you.'"

C.

When your son asks you in time to come, "What is the meaning of the testimonies and the statutes and the ordinances which the LORD our God has commanded you?" then you shall say to your son, "We were Pharaoh's slaves in Egypt; and the LORD brought us out of Egypt with a mighty hand; and the LORD showed signs and wonders, great and grievous, against Egypt and against Pharaoh and all his household, before our eyes; and he brought us out from there, that he might bring us in and give us the land which he swore to give to our fathers."

D.

You shall not give up to his master a slave who has escaped from his master to you; he shall dwell with you, in your midst, in the place which he shall choose within one of your towns, where it pleases him best; you shall not oppress him.

E.

At a lodging place on the way the LORD met him and sought to kill him. Then Zipporah took a flint and cut off her son's foreskin, and touched Moses' feet with it, and said, "Surely you are a bridegroom of blood to me!" So he let him alone.

F.

So they sent a message to Joseph, saying, "Your father gave this command before he died, 'Say to Joseph, Forgive, I pray you, the transgression of your brothers and their sin, because they did evil to you.' And now, we pray you, forgive the transgression of the servants of the God of your father." Joseph wept when they spoke to him...Joseph said to them, "Fear not, for am I in the place of God? As for you, you meant evil against me; but God meant it for good, to bring it about that many people should be kept alive, as they are today."

G.

The fathers shall not be put to death for the children, nor shall the children be put to death for the fathers; every man shall be put to death for his own sin.

H.

So I [Moses] lay prostrate before the LORD for these forty days and forty nights, because the LORD had said he would destroy you. And I prayed to the LORD, "O Lord GOD, destroy not thy people and thy heritage, whom thou has redeemed through thy greatness, whom thou has brought out of Egypt with a mighty hand. Remember thy servants, Abraham, Isaac, and Jacob; do not regard the stubbornness of this people, or their wickedness...."

Frame # 45

In the exhibit passages are collected from the Jahwist, the Elohist, and the Deuteronomist. Test your absorption of distinctions among these sources by answering the questions below. You may wish to review by using the Index at the end of this program.

1. "A" comes from the _____.

   Ideas in the passage that lead to classification _____

   _____

2. "B" comes from the _____.

   Ideas in the passage that lead to classification _____

   _____

3. "C" comes from the _____.

   Ideas in the passage that lead to classification _____

   _____

4. "D" comes from the _____.

   Ideas in the passage that lead to classification _____

   _____

5. "E" comes from the _____.

   Ideas in the passage that lead to classification _____

   _____

6. "F" comes from the _____.

   Ideas in the passage that lead to classification _____

   _____

7. "G" comes from the _____.

   Ideas in the passage that lead to classification _____

   _____

8. "H" comes from the _____.

   Ideas in the passage that lead to classification _____

   _____

1. "A" comes from the *Deuteronomist*.

   Ideas in the passage that lead to classification *Mentions fear and love of God. Also mentions total devotion--"all your heart and...all your soul."*

2. "B" comes from the *Elohist*.

   Ideas in the passage that lead to classification *Elohim reveals his name as Jahweh to Moses.*

3. "C" comes from the *Deuteronomist*.

   Ideas in the passage that lead to classification *Reminds Israel that formerly they were slaves. The land was given to Israel in order that Jahweh's oath to Israel's fathers might be fulfilled.*

4. "D" comes from the *Deuteronomist*.

   Ideas in the passage that lead to classification *A humane principle is stressed with regard to the treatment of runaway slaves.*

5. "E" comes from the *Jahwist*.

   Ideas in the passage that lead to classification *Jahweh attempts to kill Moses because Moses' son has not been circumcised--a ceremonial rule which even Moses has to obey.*

6. "F" comes from the *Elohist*.

   Ideas in the passage that lead to classification *Even though Joseph's brothers intend evil, it is Elohim who controls events and determines whether good or evil results.*

7. "G" comes from the *Deuteronomist*.

   Ideas in the passage that lead to classification *A concern that only a guilty individual be punished.*

8. "H" comes from the *Deuteronomist*.

   Ideas in the passage that lead to classification *Describes Israel as a stubborn people. Does not try to prove that Israel merits being chosen by Jahweh.*

Frames # 5-13 and 35 included references to the fourth source, the Priestly, to which we now return. Examine the selections below from the Priestly account of Creation in order to form judgements about the concept of the deity.

Genesis 1:1-8.

    In the beginning God created the heavens and the earth. The earth was without form and void, and darkness was upon the face of the deep; and the Spirit of God was moving over the face of the waters.
       And God said, "Let there be light"; and there was light. And God saw that the light was good; and God separated the light from the darkness. God called the light Day, and the darkness he called Night. And there was evening and there was morning, one day.
       And God said, "Let there be a firmament in the midst of the waters, and let it separate the waters from the waters." And God made the firmament and separated the waters which were under the firmament from the waters which were above the firmament. And it was so. And God called the firmament Heaven. And there was evening and there was morning, a second day.

Circle the numbers of statements below that make probable deductions about the passages given above.

1. Like the Jahwist, the Priestly source believes that man knew God as Jahweh from the very beginning of Creation.

2. Like the Elohist, the Priestly source believes that man used the generic term Elohim at first.

3. When it says that God "said" something, it is not necessary to suppose that the author thought of God's possessing a human form; to say that God "spoke" can be another way of expressing the thoughts of God.

4. The sequence of events set forth by the author suggests that he thought of God as bringing forth creation at random.

5. The language of the account places an accent on a planned and orderly creation.

ANSWER to Frame # 46

   2, 3, and 5 are probable deductions.

A. Genesis 1:31-2:4a.

And God saw everything that he had made, and behold, it was very good. And there was evening and there was morning, a sixth day.

Thus the heavens and the earth were finished, and all the host of them. And on the seventh day God finished his work which he had done, and he rested on the seventh day from all his work which he had done. So God blessed the seventh day and hallowed it, because on it God rested from all his work which he had done in creation.

These are the generations of the heavens and the earth when they were created.

B. Genesis 9:1-13.

And God blessed Noah and his sons, and said to them, "Be fruitful and multiply, and fill the earth. The fear of you and the dread of you shall be upon every beast of the earth, and upon every bird of the air, upon everything that creeps on the ground and all the fish of the sea; into your hand they are delivered. Every moving thing that lives shall be food for you; and as I gave you the green plants, I give you everything. Only you shall not eat flesh with its life, that is, its blood. For your lifeblood I will surely require a reckoning; of every beast I will require it and of man; of every man's brother I will require the life of man. Whoever sheds the blood of man, by man shall his blood be shed; for God made man in his own image. And you, be fruitful and multiply, bring forth abundantly on the earth and multiply in it."

Then God said to Noah and to his sons with him, "Behold, I establish my covenant with you and your descendants after you, and with every living creature that is with you, the birds, the cattle, and every beast of the earth with you, as many as came out of the ark. I establish my covenant with you, that never again shall all flesh be cut off by the waters of a flood, and never again shall there be a flood to destroy the earth." And God said, "This is the sign of the covenant which I make between me and you and every living creature that is with you, for all future generations: I set my bow in the cloud, and it shall be a sign of the covenant between me and the earth."

C. Genesis 17:1-5,7-10.

When Abram was ninety-nine years old the LORD appeared to Abram, and said to him, "I am God Almighty; walk before me, and be blameless. And I will make my covenant between me and you, and will multiply you exceedingly." Then Abram fell on his face; and God said to him, "Behold, my covenant is with you, and you shall be the father of a multitude of nations. No longer shall your name be Abram, but your name shall be Abraham; for I have made you the father of a multitude of nations....And I will establish my covenant between me and you and your descendants after you throughout their generations for an everlasting covenant, to be God to you and to your descendants after you. And I will give to you, and to your descendants after you, the land of your sojournings, all the land of Canaan, for an everlasting possession; and I will be their God."

And God said to Abraham, "As for you, you shall keep my covenant, you and your descendants after you throughout their generations. This is my covenant, which you shall keep, between me and you and your descendants after you: Every male among you shall be circumcised."

Examine the passages in the exhibit to discover some of the stylistic characteristics of the Priestly source.

In the questions that follow, the capital letters represent the passages in the exhibit.

1. A number of terms for the deity are used by the Priestly source. Place a check appropriately to indicate where a term or phrase is found.

   A   B   C

   ___ ___ ___   a. The Priestly source uses Jahweh, a term employed by the Jahwist, by the Elohist after Exodus 3:15, and by Deuteronomy.

   ___ ___ ___   b. He uses what must have been an ancient term in the Hebrew tradition, God Almighty [El Shaddai].

   ___ ___ ___   c. He uses Elohim, a term used by the Elohist *in Genesis*.

2. An important conclusion follows with respect to locating the sources simply by the use of a term for the deity. Underline the element in the following sentence that makes it a correct statement.

   In distinguishing among the materials that belong to the Jahwist, the Elohist, the Deuteronomist, and the Priestly sources one needs to know (only which term is used for the deity)(other items about the passages in addition to the term used for the deity).

3. The tone of the Priestly account tends to be stately and deliberate. Some of this impression is made by many repetitions of key phrases. Indicate below where the following phrasings are found in the passages in the exhibit, by placing checks appropriately.

   A   B   C

   ___ ___ ___   a. I [will] establish my covenant.

   ___ ___ ___   b. from all his work which he had done

   ___ ___ ___   c. be fruitful and multiply

   ___ ___ ___   d. you and your descendants after you

   ___ ___ ___   e. sign of the covenant

   ___ ___ ___   f. on the seventh day

   ___ ___ ___   g. the father of a multitude of nations

ANSWER to Frame # 47

1. A number of terms for the deity are used by the Priestly source. Place a check appropriately to indicate where a term or phrase is found.

   A   B   C

   ___ ___ ✓ a. The Priestly source uses Jahweh, a term employed by the Jahwist, by the Elohist after Exodus 3:15, and by Deuteronomy.

   ___ ___ ✓ b. He uses what must have been an ancient term in the Hebrew tradition, God Almighty [El Shaddai].

   ✓   ✓   ✓ c. He uses Elohim, a term used by the Elohist *in Genesis*.

2. An important conclusion follows with respect to locating the sources simply by the use of a term for the deity. Underline the element in the following sentence that makes it a correct statement.

   In distinguishing among the materials that belong to the Jahwist, the Elohist, the Deuteronomist, and the Priestly sources one needs to know (only which term is used for the deity)(<u>other items about the passages in addition to the term used for the deity</u>).

3. The tone of the Priestly account tends to be stately and deliberate. Some of this impression is made by many repetitions of key phrases. Indicate below where the following phrasings are found in the passages in the exhibit, by placing checks appropriately.

   A   B   C

   ___ ✓   ✓ a. I [will] establish my covenant.

   ✓   ___ ___ b. from all his work which he had done

   ___ ✓   ___ c. be fruitful and multiply

   ___ ✓   ✓ d. you and your descendants after you

   ___ ✓   ___ e. sign of the covenant

   ✓   ___ ___ f. on the seventh day

   ___ ___ ✓ g. the father of a multitude of nations

A. Genesis 1:31-2:4a.

And God saw everything that he had made, and behold, it was very good. And there was evening and there was morning, a sixth day.

Thus the heavens and the earth were finished, and all the host of them. And on the seventh day God finished his work which he had done, and he rested on the seventh day from all his work which he had done. So God blessed the seventh day and hallowed it, because on it God rested from all his work which he had done in creation.

These are the generations of the heavens and the earth when they were created.

B. Genesis 9:1-13.

And God blessed Noah and his sons, and said to them, "Be fruitful and multiply, and fill the earth. The fear of you and the dread of you shall be upon every beast of the earth, and upon every bird of the air, upon everything that creeps on the ground and all the fish of the sea; into your hand they are delivered. Every moving thing that lives shall be food for you; and as I gave you the green plants, I give you everything. Only you shall not eat flesh with its life, that is, its blood. For your lifeblood I will surely require a reckoning; of every beast I will require it and of man; of every man's brother I will require the life of man. Whoever sheds the blood of man, by man shall his blood be shed; for God made man in his own image. And you, be fruitful and multiply, bring forth abundantly on the earth and multiply in it."

Then God said to Noah and to his sons with him, "Behold, I establish my covenant with you and your descendants after you, and with every living creature that is with you, the birds, the cattle, and every beast of the earth with you, as many as came out of the ark. I establish my covenant with you, that never again shall all flesh be cut off by the waters of a flood, and never again shall there be a flood to destroy the earth." And God said, "This is the sign of the covenant which I make between me and you and every living creature that is with you, for all future generations: I set my bow in the cloud, and it shall be a sign of the covenant between me and the earth."

C. Genesis 17:1-5,7-10.

When Abram was ninety-nine years old the LORD appeared to Abram, and said to him, "I am God Almighty; walk before me, and be blameless. And I will make my covenant between me and you, and will multiply you exceedingly." Then Abram fell on his face; and God said to him, "Behold, my covenant is with you, and you shall be the father of a multitude of nations. No longer shall your name be Abram, but your name shall be Abraham; for I have made you the father of a multitude of nations....And I will establish my covenant between me and you and your descendants after you throughout their generations for an everlasting covenant, to be God to you and to your descendants after you. And I will give to you, and to your descendants after you, the land of your sojournings, all the land of Canaan, for an everlasting possession; and I will be their God."

And God said to Abraham, "As for you, you shall keep my covenant, you and your descendants after you throughout their generations. This is my covenant, which you shall keep, between me and you and your descendants after you: Every male among you shall be circumcised."

The exhibit from the previous frame has been repeated so that you can observe some special ideas presented by the Priestly source.

In the left-hand column below are found phrases used in the passages in the exhibit. In the right-hand column are found ideas which are being expressed by the quotations used.
Match a quotation with the idea it expresses by placing the letter of the matching element in the blank preceding the quotation.

____ 1. Every male among you shall be circumcised.

____ 2. So God blessed the seventh day and hallowed it, because on it God rested from all his work...

____ 3. Whoever sheds the blood of man, by man shall his blood be shed; for God made man in his own image.

____ 4. Only you shall not eat flesh with its life, that is, its blood.

____ 5. I set my bow in the cloud, and it shall be a sign of the covenant between me and the earth.

a. The rainbow is thought of as a symbol of the covenant that God makes never again to destroy his creation by flood.

b. Man is forbidden to take human life.

c. Blood cannot be consumed, for blood is the "life" of flesh.

d. The Sabbath is made sacred by the fact that God chose to rest on the seventh day.

e. All male descendants of Abraham are to be circumcised.

6. The Priestly source in Genesis and Exodus sets forth a scheme of progressive gifts that God makes his creation. Place a check before the arrangement that correctly indicates in what order this series of progressive gifts actually appears in the Priestly source.

____ a. the covenant with the people of Israel at Sinai at which Jahweh
        through Moses indicated that Israel would be his holy people
   the hallowing of the Sabbath
   the covenant with Noah
   the covenant with Abraham

____ b. the hallowing of the Sabbath
   the covenant with Noah
   the covenant with Abraham
   the covenant with the people of Israel at Sinai at which Jahweh
        through Moses indicated that Israel would be his holy people

____ c. the covenant with Abraham
   the hallowing of the Sabbath
   the covenant with the people of Israel at Sinai at which Jahweh
        through Moses indicated that Israel would be his holy people
   the covenant with Noah

_e_ 1. Every male among you
shall be circumcised.

_d_ 2. So God blessed the
seventh day and hallowed
it, because on it God rested
from all his work...

_b_ 3. Whoever sheds the blood
of man, by man shall his
blood be shed; for God
made man in his own image.

_c_ 4. Only you shall not eat
flesh with its life, that
is, its blood.

_c_ 5. I set my bow in the cloud,
and it shall be a sign of the
covenant between me and the
earth.

a. The rainbow is thought of as a
symbol of the covenant that God
makes never again to destroy his
creation by flood.

b. Man is forbidden to take human
life.

c. Blood cannot be consumed, for
blood is the "life" of flesh.

d. The Sabbath is made sacred by
the fact that God chose to rest
on the seventh day.

e. All male descendants of Abraham
are to be circumcised.

6. The Priestly source in Genesis and Exodus sets forth a scheme of progressive
gifts that God makes his creation. Place a check before the arrangement that
correctly indicates in what order this series of progressive gifts actually
appears in the Priestly source.

____ a. the covenant with the people of Israel at Sinai at which Jahweh
         through Moses indicated that Israel would be his holy people
      the hallowing of the Sabbath
      the covenant with Noah
      the covenant with Abraham

✓ b. the hallowing of the Sabbath
      the covenant with Noah
      the covenant with Abraham
      the covenant with the people of Israel at Sinai at which Jahweh
         through Moses indicated that Israel would be his holy people

____ c. the covenant with Abraham
      the hallowing of the Sabbath
      the covenant with the people of Israel at Sinai at which Jahweh
         through Moses indicated that Israel would be his holy people
      the covenant with Noah

Leviticus 19:1-18.

And the LORD said to Moses, "Say to all the congregation of the people of
Israel, You shall be holy; for I the LORD your God am holy. Every one of
you shall revere his mother and his father, and you shall keep my sabbaths:
I am the LORD your God. Do not turn to idols or make for yourselves molten
gods: I am the LORD your God.
    "When you offer a sacrifice of peace offerings to the LORD, you shall
offer it so that you may be accepted. It shall be eaten the same day you
offer it, or on the morrow; and anything left over until the third day
shall be burned with fire. If it is eaten at all on the third day, it is
an abomination; it will not be accepted, and every one who eats it shall
bear his iniquity, because he has profaned a holy thing of the LORD; and
that person shall be cut off from his people.
    "When you reap the harvest of your land, you shall not reap your field
to its very border, neither shall you gather the gleanings after your
harvest. And you shall not strip your vineyard bare, neither shall you
gather the fallen grapes of your vineyard; you shall leave them for the
poor and the sojourner: I am the LORD your God.
    "You shall not steal, nor deal falsely, nor lie to one another.
And you shall not swear by my name falsely, and so profane the name of
your God: I am the LORD.
    "You shall not oppress your neighbor or rob him. The wages of a
hired servant shall not remain with you all night until the morning.
You shall not curse the deaf or put a stumbling block before the blind,
but you shall fear your God: I am the LORD.
    "You shall do no injustice in judgment, you shall not be partial to
the poor or defer to the great, but in righteousness shall you judge your
neighbor. You shall not go up and down as a slanderer among your people,
and you shall not stand forth against the life of your neighbor: I am the
LORD.
    "You shall not hate your brother in your heart, but you shall reason
with your neighbor, lest you bear sin because of him. You shall not take
vengeance or bear any grudge against the sons of your own people, but
you shall love your neighbor as yourself: I am the LORD."

In Exodus, Leviticus, and Numbers [Leviticus and Numbers are Priestly material] you could predict that the Priestly source would be expressing ceremonial matters; ceremonial laws form a ruling interest for any priestly school of thought.
But inspect the exceptional passage given in the exhibit in order to uncover the ethical interests also to be found.

In the left-hand column below, "C" stands for <u>ceremonial</u> issues; in the right-hand column "E" stands for <u>ethical</u> issues. Classify the rules given by placing appropriate checks.

Rules that have appeared in other sources now reappearing in P [Priestly source].

  C   E

___ ___ 1. Mother and father are to be revered.

___ ___ 2. The Sabbaths are to be kept.

___ ___ 3. No images are to be created.

___ ___ 4. Provision is to be made for the poor by allowing them to glean grain and fruit. Such gleanings do not belong to the landowner.

___ ___ 5. Don't steal, deal falsely, or lie.

___ ___ 6. Don't profane the name of Jahweh.

___ ___ 7. Don't keep the wages of a hired servant overnight.

___ ___ 8. Don't mistreat the disadvantaged.

___ ___ 9. Give exact justice, deferring neither to the poor nor to the rich.

Rules appearing for the first time.

___ ___ 10. A sacrifice of peace offerings must be eaten on the same day or, at the latest, on the next day.

___ ___ 11. Don't engage in slander.

___ ___ 12. Don't hate anyone.

___ ___ 13. Love your neighbor as yourself.

Underline the elements that produce correct statements below.

    14. In the special chapter from Leviticus there are more (ethical than ceremonial rules)(ceremonial than ethical rules).

    15. A high ethical principle is stated: that the relationship between men should be governed by (love)(self-interest).

Rules that have appeared in other sources now reappearing in P [Priestly source].

C   E

___ ✓ 1. Mother and father are to be revered. *If you agree with many students who placed checks in both columns, this could not be called mistaken.*

✓ ___ 2. The Sabbaths are to be kept.

✓ ___ 3. No images are to be created.

___ ✓ 4. Provision is to be made for the poor by allowing them to glean grain and fruit. Such gleanings do not belong to the landowner.

___ ✓ 5. Don't steal, deal falsely, or lie.

✓ ___ 6. Don't profane the name of Jahweh.

___ ✓ 7. Don't keep the wages of a hired servant overnight.

___ ✓ 8. Don't mistreat the disadvantaged.

___ ✓ 9. Give exact justice, deferring neither to the poor nor to the rich.

Rules appearing for the first time.

✓ ___ 10. A sacrifice of peace offerings must be eaten on the same day or, at the latest, on the next day.

___ ✓ 11. Don't engage in slander.

___ ✓ 12. Don't hate anyone.

___ ✓ 13. Love your neighbor as yourself.

14. In the special chapter from Leviticus there are more (<u>ethical than ceremonial rules</u>)(ceremonial than ethical rules).

15. A high ethical principle is stated: that the relationship between men should be governed by (<u>love</u>)(self-interest).

A.

Then the LORD God formed man of dust from the ground, and breathed into his nostrils the breath of life; and man became a living being.

B.

Not because of your righteousness or the uprightness of your heart are you going in to possess their land; but because of the wickedness of these nations the LORD your God is driving them out from before you.

C.

And God said, "Let there be light"; and there was light. And God saw that the light was good; and God separated the light from the darkness. God called the light Day, and the darkness he called Night. And there was evening and there was morning, one day.

D.

Know then in your heart that, as a man disciplines his son, the LORD your God disciplines you.

E.

Then Noah built an altar to the LORD, and took of every clean animal and of every clean bird, and offered burnt offerings on the altar. And when the LORD smelled the pleasing odor, the LORD said in his heart, "I will never again curse the ground because of man..."

F.

Fear not, for am I in the place of God? As for you, you meant evil against me; but God meant it for good, to bring it about that many people should be kept alive, as they are today. So do not fear; I will provide for you and your little ones. Thus he reassured them and comforted them.

G.

And the LORD turned a very strong west wind, which lifted the locusts and drove them into the Red Sea; not a single locust was left in all the country of Egypt. But the LORD hardened Pharaoh's heart, and he did not let the children of Israel go.

H.

The LORD saw that the wickedness of man was great in the earth, and that every imagination of the thoughts of his heart was only evil continually. And the LORD was sorry that he had made man on the earth, and it grieved him to his heart. So the LORD said, "I will blot out man whom I have created from the face of the ground..."

In the exhibit passages are collected from all four sources. Test your absorption of distinctions among the sources by answering the questions below.

"A" comes from the _____.

Ideas in the passage that lead to classification _____

_____

"B" comes from the _____.

Ideas in the passage that lead to classification _____

_____

"C" comes from the _____.

Ideas in the passage that lead to classification _____

_____

"D" comes from the _____.

Ideas in the passage that lead to classification _____

_____

"E" comes from the _____.

Ideas in the passage that lead to classification _____

_____

"F" comes from the _____.

Ideas in the passage that lead to classification _____

_____

"G" comes from the _____.

Ideas in the passage that lead to classification _____

_____

"H" comes from the _____.

Ideas in the passage that lead to classification _____

_____

"A" comes from the *Jahwist*.

Ideas in the passage that lead to classification *One of the two creation stories and this uses Jahweh Elohim--a mark of the Jahwist. Human-like actions.*

"B" comes from the *Deuteronomist*.

Ideas in the passage that lead to classification *Israel is being used for God's purposes, but not because Israel is good.*

"C" comes from the *Priestly source*.

Ideas in the passage that lead to classification *One of the two creation stories and this uses Elohim--the work of the Priestly source. Creation is good and is produced in an orderly way. Remember that the Elohist <u>lacks</u> an account of Creation.*

"D" comes from the *Deuteronomist*.

Ideas in the passage that lead to classification *A comment on the problem of unjust suffering and the Deuteronomist is the only one of the four sources to concern itself with this problem.*

"E" comes from the *Jahwist*.

Ideas in the passage that lead to classification *Uses human characteristics for the deity and uses Jahweh in Genesis.*

"F" comes from the *Elohist*.

Ideas in the passage that lead to classification *God is all powerful and works through the motivations of men to accomplish his own good. Uses Elohim in this Joseph story in Genesis.*

"G" comes from the *Elohist*.

Ideas in the passage that lead to classification *Since the deity is all-powerful he can make Pharaoh obstinate. Jahweh is the term for the deity but the Elohist can use Jahweh in Exodus.*

"H" comes from the *Jahwist*.

Ideas in the passage that lead to classification *Uses human characteristics for the deity in that Jahweh is "sorry" and since this story is in Genesis it is important that Jahweh is the term for the deity.*

INDEX

CEREMONIAL RULES

circumcision of Moses' son - # 21
distinguished from ethical rules - 21,22,23,34
Deuteronomist's interest - 37,38
Priestly source - 49
Ten Commandments - 23,25,34

DEITY

generic and specific terms - 6,8,9,12,15,28,31
terms in the Jahwist, Elohist, and Priestly sources - 29
terms in stories of Creation - 5
translation of Hebrew terms - 7

DEUTERONOMIST SOURCE

Chosen nation, concept given critique - 44
ethical sensitivities - 40
individual's importance - 40,42
intensity demanded in obedience to laws - 41
liturgy of Jahweh's relationship to Israel - 44
motivations for obedience to laws - 41
problem of unjust suffering - 42,43
reform in places for sacrifice - 37
relation of source to reign of Josiah - 38,39
Ten Commandments compared with the Elohist's Ten Commandments - 36

ELOHIST SOURCE

Abraham and the sacrifice of Isaac - 33
Abraham says Sarah is his sister - 26,31
Abraham with Sarah and Abimelech - 26,31,32
ceremonial rules - 25,34
deity, power of - 19,32
      terms for - 28,29,30,33,36
dreams as means by which the deity speaks to man - 31
ethical rules - 25,34,39
heroes of Israel portrayed in a more ethical/humane light - 26,28,31,33
Joseph and his brothers - 19,32
places for sacrifice - 37
Sarah's attitude toward Hagar and Hagar's son - 28
special theory that Elohim revealed himself as Jahweh to Moses - 30
Ten Commandments, compared with Deuteronomist's Ten Commandments - 36
                compared with Jahwist's Ten Commandments - 25,34

ETHICAL RULES

distinguished from ceremonial rules - 21,34
in Priestly source - 49
in Ten Commandments - 25,34